Patches
of my
Life 21-80

Includes a Collections of my Original Song Lyrics

Patches
of my
Life 21-80

Includes a Collections of my Original Song Lyrics

Kenneth Fly

Gotham Books

30 N Gould St.
Ste. 20820, Sheridan, WY 82801
https://gothambooksinc.com/

Phone: 1 (307) 464-7800

© 2025 *Kenneth Fly*. All rights reserved.

No part of this book may be reproduced, stored in a retrieval system, or transmitted by any means without the written permission of the author.

Published by Gotham Books (May 16, 2025)

ISBN: 979-8-3492-4046-1 (P)
ISBN: 979-8-3492-4047-8 (E)

Because of the dynamic nature of the Internet, any web addresses or links contained in this book may have changed since publication and may no longer be valid.

The views expressed in this work are solely those of the author and do not necessarily reflect the views of the publisher, and the publisher hereby disclaims any responsibility for them.

Patches Credits

So many people had an involvement in my life story; too many to mention, but I must name a few:

Above all the rest to the lady who gives me strength and encouragement every day throughout my life - my beautiful and wonderful wife, Samantha.

My daughter, Lori My son, Jonathan

Friend and employee, Candy Richard Radio show MC, Paul Jones

Sound: Gene Harris, Allen Huber Video: J.D. Spivey

Many other employees over the years which are too many to mention: My right hand builder, Tom Hunt

The cabin pickers:

Doug Barns Tom Hunt John Posey John Anderson

Anthony Hatfield Pete Carter Charles Tobitt

Special thanks to Dave and Judith Carney for help with putting this book together.

Table of Contents

Patches Credits v
Foreword viii
Chapter 1: ARMY DAYS 1
Chapter 2: THIS TIME I SCREWED UP 5
Chapter 3: ONE THING AFTER ANOTHER FIRE FIGHTING IN THE SWAMP 8
Chapter 4: GREAT PLACE TO MEET BEAUTIFUL LADIES 13
Chapter 5: DISCHARGED AND STRAIGHT TO WORK 15
Chapter 6: THE LADY THAT ALLOWED ME TO CHANGE MY LIFE 20
Chapter 7: THE BIG STORM 22
Chapter 8: THE TRAIN WRECK 23
Chapter 9: THE MOVE TO TENNESSEE 25
Chapter 10: OUR FIRST BORN 28
Chapter 11: OUR SECOND BIG MOVE 29
Chapter 12: MOVE FROM JOHNSON CITY TO SHELBYVILLE 32
Chapter 13: THE BIRTH OF OUR SECOND CHILD 35
Chapter 14: SAMANTHA'S TUMOR 37
Chapter 15: MOVE CLOSER TO TULLAHOMA 39
Chapter 16: MOVE TO MOORE COUNTY 41
Chapter 17: MUSIC HISTORY 42
Chapter 18: THE MUSIC STORE 44
Chapter 19: UNCLE BUNT STEPHENS DAY 45
Chapter 20: THE FIRST FOOD WAGON 47
Chapter 21: THE SECOND FOOD WAGON 48
Chapter 22: THE MOVE INSIDE 49
Chapter 23: THE RADIO SHOW 51
Chapter 24: A LITTLE TRAVEL WAS GOOD 52
Chapter 25: MY BUSINESS POLICIES 55
Chapter 26: THE OLD NEW LOG CABIN 59

Chapter 27: THEN ALONG CAME COVID-19 62
Chapter 28: STILL UP TO A CHALLENGE 64
Summary 65
Index of Songs 72

All Songs written by Ken Fly, BMI. All rights reserved.

Foreword

Patches of My Life, 21-80

A few years ago I started writing about things that has happened in my life in short story form and finally in 2013 I finished the first 24 years which was published in book form in early 2014.

This writing was entitled "Patches of My Life" which was a suggestion of a sister of mine while trying to come up with a name.

Thanks Dorothy.

Although I knew I didn't have time to complete the second part of my experiences in life, I had several requests to do just that. I sat down with my computer keyboard in front of me while the TV was either on the movie channel and Samantha, my wife of 47 years, was watching a movie that I really wasn't interested in; or it was on the news channel after which all seem to run together. You may want to call this multi-tasking, or you might have some other choice words to call it never-the-less I began to recall parts of my life starting in the early 60s.

After several reviews of the first book, I decided to follow the same format that was used in it, being short story form.

In my first writings, I went into some detail about my days in the US Military but I left some things out for various reasons. I feel now is the time to pick up there and fill in some of the spaces before continuing on to the more adult portion of my life.

I am so very proud to be part of a long line of Americans who have stood up and said "I will serve." My family has defended our nation all the way from my great great grandfather, to Charles Dequuasie who fought in the Revolutionary War to my grandson, Andrew Fly, who is presently serving.

My Family Military History

- Kenneth D. Fly, US Army 1962 - 1965 myself
- Richard N. Fly, US Navy, Peace Time, my brother
- Donald E. Fly, US Marine, Peace Time, my brother
- Edward L. Fly, US Navy, World War II, my brother
- Thomas J. Fly, US Army, World War I, my father, wounded in action
- Ella Fly, US Army, World War I, my aunt
- Andrew Young, Confederate soldier, my great uncle, prisoner of war
- John Fly, Confederate soldier, my great uncle, prisoner of war
- Robert Young, Revolutionary War, my great-great grandfather
- William Dequasie, US Army, War of 1812, my great, great, great grandfather
- Charles Dequasie, Revolutionary War, my great, great, great grandfather, was present at the battle of Yorktown
- Alexander Frame, my grandson, US Air Force
  - Andrew Fly, my grandson, US Army, Active Duty

To be able to say "he (or she) served" is the greatest compliment that can ever be said of an American.

Chapter 1

ARMY DAYS

With my number coming up for the draft, I enlisted in the US Army and went directly to training camp in South Carolina. After finding they had sent me to the wrong place, they forwarded me on to Fort Gordon, Georgia for my thirteen weeks of basic training, which paid whopping seventy-eight dollars a month. This was in October 1962 and our unit was a mixture of southern boys, northern boys, farm boys, city boys, cowboys and everything in-between. This mixture of young men, some of who had been drafted and some, like myself, had joined so we could pick our duty station and MOS (military occupational specialty). This very diverse group of men (boys) as you can imagine, lead to some very interesting situations. Some do not deserve remembering much less writing about. On the other hand some need to be preserved by writing them down.

Young and ignorant or just stupid

At an early age, I fell into the trap that a lot of young men fall into, which was and is a life lesson known as love. As most wrong marriages do, this ended in divorce and was one more life lesson learned the hard way. Being in the Army and stationed in Virginia with a wife living somewhere else who was not disciplined or loyal for that matter. As the saying goes, love is blind and had that not been true I would have known marriage would never work so with her desire to get away from home and lack of awareness this ended up in divorce, correcting a situation that never should happened in the first place. Enough about that. This behind me now, I could get on with the rest of my life.

The basic training in an army training camp was rather rugged and was designed to take away the normal thought process of a young man from most any walk of life and rebuild them with a combat attitude which would make them more likely to survive situations of war. At that time, we didn't serve as combat soldiers; rather, we were assigned to the jobs that were looked upon as our best attributes. Long periods of holding your M1 rifle over your head to duck walking while policing the grounds, a term used to mean ground such as gum paper or even match sticks in the unit area. Long marches to the overnight areas with full pack up to twelve miles with little or no rest.

Our first sergeant was a real soldier, a survivor of Pork Chop Hill combat in Korea with years of training troops and had no regard for your opinion of him. Making friends was not one of his goals. He stood before us and said his goal was for everyone to hate him before we left the training camp, and he sure made that happen. I didn't put his name here, even though I will never forget it.

Our DI (drill instructor) was a tall black sergeant in the best physical shape of anyone I had ever seen. He could run backwards all day long, going from the back of the line to the front with a collar of a straggling solder in each hand singing cadence all the way.

The training was good for all of us and especially for those who were slated to pick up a rifle and go to a war zone.

Many interesting things happened while in basic that those of us who were there will never forget. Life time friends were made, although we all went our separate ways.

I went on to train in the field of electronics having to do with the repair of radar and the operation of the Army air defense Hercules missile system. This training took me to Fort Bliss Texas and McGregor range in New Mexico.

After completing the extra training, I was sent to Deep Creek Virginia to a site designed to protect the Norfolk area from attack from air or sea.

As a member of the US Army Air Defense System, I was required to have a top secret security clearance, which I acquired with little difficulty, as I had never been involved in anything unlawful enough to cause a problem.

Being raised on a farm and following the construction business as an electrician after graduation from high school, I was in very good physical condition so I had little problem with basic training. I really felt for the guys that had an easy life before the basic training because it was tough at times.

I weighed 146 pounds when I entered the training and 172 pounds when I left Ft. Gordon, Georgia. Many changes have occurred over the years and one of them was my waist line. I held on to the twenty nine inch waist for several years but in my thirties that all became history, like most people I know.

I have always had a love for music of many kinds and that played a big part in my past time activity as a soldier.

During the time I was stationed at B Battery I was always involved with things other than operating or maintaining radar such as operating the small PX (post exchange) and running the dark room, following my interest in photography. To test our missiles, we went to McGregor Range in New Mexico and, of course, we had to make the trip to the border town of Mexico. Not the same any more either.

The border of Mexico at that time was rather unsettled and a little bit rough to say the least. Open bars. Prostitution, music groups playing in the streets for change, bull fights, etc.

To go across the border didn't cost anything and no check point. Coming back across to the United States cost two cents. The bridge was where we crossed and no one would dare to take a vehicle because no insurance was good in Mexico. As we crossed the bridge, the Mexican boys would be in the Rio Grande river waiting for someone to throw enough coins for then to catch, mostly pennies, as they would dive down, pick them up off the bottom and come up to, hold the coin up to show you they got it.

If a person was arrested in Mexico they went directly to jail and when they got out they only had the clothes on their backs. All other belongings became the property of the jailer. Cash, watch, glasses, tobacco or whatever they had.

If a military person was arrested in Mexico the US military had to get them out. Of course this was not a good thing to happen so most of us tried hard to keep our nose clean while there. Although there was always some poor soul who got loaded and messed up. It was well known that more than clothes were left in Mexico after being arrested.

Due to some special training I ended up on what we called the high power radar and at the time was the only trained person in the battery which often lead to an interesting situation. The battery commander called me in to his office and informed me that he had some bad news and he had some good news. What is the bad news I asked, he said "you are on orders for Berlin, Germany" which was not a favorable place to be at that time. What was the good news I asked and he replied "you are not going, I can't afford for you to go, so I got you off orders. I was glad.

Chapter 2

THIS TIME I SCREWED UP

We were always signing out on our time off and going to Norfolk or some other place within 50 miles which was the allowed range without an official leave order.

During peace time we were hardly ever called back to base when we were off duty.

It was Thanksgiving weekend and I had no duty scheduled that weekend so, as I had done before; I decided I would sign out and travel home to be with my family at my mother's home in North Carolina. My only means of travel was to ride my thumb (hitch hike), so off I went. Home was about an eight hour trip if things went well. I made it home without a problem and as you might recall, if you were around in 1963, that weekend went down in history due to the assassination of President John Kennedy. Well, being in the type unit I was in, we were naturally called up to emergency status because nobody knew what would come next or who was behind this event.

Now being in North Carolina, eight hours from base without the proper leave order or weekend pass, was not a good place to be when the battery was called up on emergency status. I knew as soon as I saw the news on TV I was likely in trouble, but what was I to do? I called the orderly room at the battery and they said "where are you, the captain made recall check and you are the only person not accounted for". I said "put me through to him". When he came to the phone he wanted to know where I was and how long would it take to get back to the site. I told him what I had done and, if lucky, I would be back in eight hours.

As luck would have it I knew a sailor that I had caught a ride with a time or two before, who was stationed in Norfolk. He was in Charlotte which was about thirty miles away so I called and he had come home on a three day pass but had to return to the ship due to the shooting of the President. He picked me up in Monroe and off we went to Virginia. Our time getting back was very good. When I came in the orderly room door, the Captain was waiting very calmly. He said report to your duty station and be in my office at 08:00 in the morning.

I have always been thankful for his professional manner and of handling my screw up. To make the story short, I was charged with being AWOL and got an Article 15 for which I got restricted to post for fourteen days and some extra guard duty. Not nearly as bad as it could have been if we had a real national emergency. Lesson learned and never again did I take leave on my own without a pass.

Dust up with the Judge

People who knew me during this part of my life would tell you that I was always a rather speedy driver and my car at that time was a 1953 Buick Special. As I recall, I had been on an evening out in the town just down from the missile site where I was assigned. I had been playing music at a small bar which was a normal activity on most nights off. After the evening music gig I was returning to the base and as I started to pull into the highway to return to the base, I saw an Army staff car, a 1957 Chevy, and a specialist fourth class from the base was driving. He said my old Buick can't hang with his Chevy staff car. The race was on. We had just got up to speed when a local police officer fell in behind us and now the race was really on.

The access road to the base was about a quarter of a mile long and connected to the main highway. Route 17 was the main, and actually the only entrance, to the base by way of a guard gate.

If a service man was stopped by the police in that area they were known to be rather rough on them which caused some animosity between the law enforcement community and the military. As a rule, if a car came up the access road, and the guard could tell who it was, the first gate would open and allow the car to enter. If a car made it past the gate, it was on government property and the civilian police had no way to make an arrest or attach an automobile.

In our case, since it was so late at night, the guard was walking the fence, leaving no one to open the gate, so we had to stop. While we were stopped waiting to enter, the trooper made his arrest, and for the charge of speeding we spent the night in jail in Portsmouth, Virginia, and the fine was $107.75. In 1962, that was a lot of money for a serviceman who was drawing $80.00 a month.

Lieutenant Snellings was the officer of the day and he came and got us out of the jail. We were glad the Captain wasn't the guy that came to get us, as LT Snellings was a nice guy and a friend.

A lesson well learned because that was the last time I spent any time in the clink.

The reason I named this story the dust up with the judge was it is not a normal thing to be taken to jail for speeding but in this case I was an Army guy. As I found out later the Judge had a bad experience, a few years back, when his wife was killed in an auto accident by a sailor from the Norfolk area. It was said that the judge had it in for any serviceman that came to his court.

During the time I was playing music, I ran into some real characters. I learned that the boys I was with were taking what was known back then as Bennies. Knowing that if I was known to be around this kind of crowd, it would put my security clearance in jeopardy. So I did the best thing I knew to do and stopped playing music and sold all my instruments and amps.

Being a person who had to be doing something all the time with many interests, this attitude led me to do several things such as operate the photo lab and the small post exchange which took the place of playing music every night.

Chapter 3

ONE THING AFTER ANOTHER FIRE FIGHTING IN THE SWAMP

Being in the service exposed me to several things and put me in some situations that I probably wouldn't have gotten into as a civilian.

Working in the swamp

For example the dismal swamp was just across the inland water way from the base. One day we were told that the swamp was on fire and volunteers were needed to go into the swamp and help stop the spread of the fire.

The local fire department and other volunteers had been in the swamp for several days before we were called in, so there was a lot of smoldering moss and lots of smoke in the area. We used our masks and air tanks where we were in the worst areas. A swamp fire is mostly burning the pet moss under the surface of the ground, which was several feet deep. As you moved along the ground with the under surface smoldering you were likely to fall through the top layer of solid ground into the burning moss which could be rather deep.

In the area of the fire there were patches of low wet areas with some water channels. Water pumps were placed into the channels and hoses were hand held in order to extinguish the fires.

This firefighting effort went on for twenty four hours, seven days a week until under control.

The night shift, that we were assigned to, gave us a sense of uncertainty. The swamp had several types of animals and snakes, one being the rattle snake. I recall we were in an area that had been burning for some time and as the under-lying moss burned the top layer would drop down and cause anything in that area to move. In the case of the snakes the rattler would make his presence known with the natural alarm, his rattler. Not being able to see much with the smoke, and only using a light mounted on your head, the feeling of concern grew greater.

The cabin in the swamp

Another thing that happened with the swamp was that I had a friend that was an officer in the National Guard and he had found a small island about a mile and half deep in the swamp suitable for a small cabin. He took all the building materials in by boat. One day he asked if I would like to see the cabin and I said sure because I really didn't really believe all I had heard about it,

He had a flat bottom boat, with a five horse outboard motor on it, so it took a while to get to the cabin. It was spring of the year and the water snakes were mating, which was an experience. The snakes were in a big ball on a low hanging limb. We took the time to stop and get a closer look at them when the officer reached down in the boat and got a short twelve gauge shotgun and took a shot at the snakes. They went everywhere. What a sight and not a pleasant one at that.

Past time and extra money

Our army unit was small with only limited personnel which caused us to be a rather close knit unit. We were located in the middle of a corn field with a radar area and just down the road was a launching area. Not much to do on site but watch TV, play music or play cards and shoot pool. We did have a small post exchange.

Specialist 4 Wilson from Alabama, who worked as a generator operator, and I were the Post Exchange operators. By doing so we made a little extra money. Being a PX operator qualified us to be licensed to operate whatever type of vehicle that was on post so we could go to Fort Monroe and bring back supplies. We would open the PX every day long enough for everybody to get supplies. We were authorized to sell 3.2 percent beer on post but we knew the color stamps for the 6 percent beer and loaded in as much as we could get away with. Of course we could get more for the stronger beer because we had several beer drinkers on site. I guess you might say we kinda played the system.

Before knowing about the radar range

We were always trying new things and the whole experience was a learning curve for all of us. Keep in mind the time frame and those microwave ovens were not out yet. One day we decided that if our training was true and that if we were to get in front of the radar cone while it was turned on it would result in serious injury, sterilization or even death. So we decided to conduct an experiment. We went to the mess hall and got a steak, tied it to the radar cone, turned it on to see if it would cook it. Making the mistake of turning the rotation on also we found did it not only cook the steak but slung grease all over the place. With an inspection due in a few days we spent all our off time cleaning the grease off the radar. Needless to say we didn't try that again but we did find out direct radar rays will cook a steak.

Another big change for the military

In 1963 (the old army) homosexuals were looked at as a threat to national defense, and if found out were kicked out of the service. This very thing happened to a captain. In our unit this was treated as a big deal and anyone having direct dealings with him were part of the investigation, I am sure I will never forget that event. I added this note just to place a mark in history as one of those changes that will never return to what some see as normal

Who shot the deer

Although we were a secret security site some things happened that you would never think would. A deer was shot by one guard from one of the radar towers and was cleaned behind the mess hall and eaten by the troops. Our mess sergeant was a good cook and would trade the supplies from the army to the local farmers for fresh eggs, milk and other foods.

Interesting people

I'll just call him Sam. Sam was quite a corrector and gave us all a lot of laughs. One evening Sam got hold of a pump fire extinguisher and shot out all the post lights on the access road. He had a run in with several of the officers and stayed on KP most of the time.

Sam was in charge of the officer's mess and to polish the floor we used a large machine that had a handle with a switch that started the motion, which was a round polishing pad on the bottom. This particular machine had a bad switch and was taped on the on position so when you plugged it in it started rotating. With the pad stuck on the floor the long handle would start spinning round in about in a four foot circle. As I said before Sam was quite a trickster and on this day he stayed true to his character. The chaplain was a large black captain and he seemed to always come in to eat after the other officers which created a bigger mess for Sam to clean up. When the opportunity presented itself Sam plugged the faulty floor polisher just in time for the captain to have to make a fast move to keep from being hit by the moving handle spilling food on the floor. The reaction of the captain was of disgust and in his own way Sam said "sounds like you got a personal problem you need to speak to the chaplain". Well, enough about Sam.

Nags Head

A car load of us guys went to Nags Head on the outer banks of North Carolina. In the early sixties there were no bridges to some of the islands so we had to take the ferry boat. Oh yea, Sam was driving an old Oldsmobile so we took his car. That old heavy car was not one that should have been on the beach, but we took it out there, anyway. I am sure that a video of six guys working to get a car out of the sand before the tide came in would have been a winner but of course there were no video cameras in the bunch.

Nags Head was a good place to go scuba diving around the old sunken ships. We enjoyed that outing as often as we could. Williams, Vaughn, Boutleer, Gilbert and a couple others enjoyed the graveyard of the Atlantic. The high light of this was to play with the dolphins, but it was time to get out of there when the sharks showed up.

Smooth ride

You hardly ever saw anyone on the beach along parts of the outer banks. The sand was hard and wide, making an ideal place to ride motorcycles. Moving along at one hundred miles an hour on the beach was quite a thrill for a young GI. Now that was a foolish thing to do, but youth has a way of doing foolish things, I suppose. It was a 1952 Harley, Davidson 74 pan head in beautiful shape. One of the highlights of my time in the Army.

Virginia Beach was another of the great places to go. Upman had a Corvair convertible which sure did catch the eye of some good-looking girls.

Chapter 4

GREAT PLACE TO MEET BEAUTIFUL LADIES

The story is that I also stood on the seat while riding in and out of the white line on the highway. I am not admitting that, just saying that is the stories they tell. Wilson brought it up after 35 years when he visited me in Tennessee.

With the help of relatives

I had a cousin who, at that time, was rather well off and had accumulated his wealth in the house moving business. He moved buildings of all kinds so in an effort to make a little extra money; I went to work for him when I was off duty.

I had been around the construction business as an electrician before entering the army and fit in well with his line of work. He offered to give me a crew and help me go in the moving business after I was discharged from service. But life's events changed my path and I never returned to peruse this venture.

Fun past time but risky

As I said before one of my life interests was music and playing guitar so when I could I would get involved where ever possible. Met a guy by the name of Rex who had a country band and played in a few night spots. After a few sessions he asked me to join the group, so I did. We were called Rex and the swinging three.

Didn't take long to figure out these guys were not where I should be and possibly put my military clearance in jeopardy. As it was and is with a lot of music groups the smoke and pills were a part of life but weren't for me so I backed out of the group. These guys were great musicians and played my kind of music. I frequently sat in with them after that but never got involved with other groups, and in fact sold all my gear to stay away from the temptation.

Our unit's objective was to guard the east coast, while stationed in Virginia and Chicago area and when in Indiana, from any threat from land, air, or water for that matter with the use of Nike Hercules missiles. As I said earlier, everything was so secret so we didn't talk about it for several years for fear of violating our code.

Although I was offered an increase in rank to stay in after three years I had enough of the military and was honorably discharged in Gary, Indiana. I just wasn't cut out to put up with the military way of doing things. It has been said that there are three ways of doing a few things: the right way, the wrong way, and the military way.

We were not aware of it but plans were being made for the National Guard to take over the site in Virginia. Soon we were training the Guard to operate and maintain the radar and missile launching operation for the Army. We were a close unit and were mostly like brothers, so it was a rather sad departure for some of us.

My new assignment was to be in Munster, Indiana which was just south of Hammond, Indiana and southwest of Chicago which was our charge to keep safe from attack.

Chapter 5

DISCHARGED AND STRAIGHT TO WORK

While stationed at Munster, I lived off post and finished out my tour of duty there. Discharged in Gary, Indiana, and went to work for the Erie Lackawanna Rail Road. They hired me because of my experience in electrical wiring and electronics in the Army. This put me in line to work for the signal department, as a new signal system was being installed later that year. So I could go straight to work. I was given a job as a Teletype operator running consist of trains. I also was a tower operator running trains out of the Hammond yard. The tower operator's job was to operate the switches and watch the trains by to see that everything was ok with no flat wheels or shifted cargo. As there were no radios or walkie talkies, we had to write notes, called orders, to the engineer and trainman on the caboose. These notes were attached to a loop string and the trainmen would scoop them up as they went by the tower. The tower operator was in constant contact with the dispatcher several miles away by open phone lines.

I finally went to work on the job I was hired for.

One of the jobs of the signal maintainer was to take care of the crossing lights and crossing arms anywhere a street crossed the tracks. Some of the system ran through the city of Hammond, Indiana and some trains were quite long and held up traffic for a while at times. This being the case, if a driver saw a train coming, rather than get stopped, would try to go around the crossing arms and break the cross arms. It was the job of the signal maintainer to replace or repair the arms because they were equipped with flasher lights.

About once a month an automobile would get hit by a train and in many cases this resulted in death. In this case, the first person that was called was the maintainer because it was his job to check all signals and flashers, write a report for the ICC, and lock it in the signal case for the police inspector. Being one of the first people on the scene, we ran into some rather troubling and gruesome situations.

Having a background of electricity in civilian life and electronics in the army radar systems, I applied for a job with the Erie Lackawanna Rail Road in Hammond, Indiana as a signal maintainer. The Rail Road was going to a new welded rail system and needed someone for the new circuitry. So with my experience I got the job, and at that time was the youngest signal maintainer with the company.

Weed

I learned a lot while on the railroad. Sometimes I would fill in for a friend and run the consist on trains and operate the teletype machine. I also worked as a tower operator running train signals for trains coming out of Hammond Yard; I also ran the tower over the draw bridge where all the trains going to Chicago came across the Little Calumet River. Just across the river and still under the RR draw bridge we kept seeing hobos jump off the north bound trains and go into the junk yard. They would build a camp fire and stay for a day or so. One day we noticed that every once in a while one of the hobos would go down to the river which was grown up with thick weeds and bushes. We decided to see what they were doing next to the river and boy, what a surprise we got; the marijuana weed was at least eight feet tall and lots and lots of it. We decided that the hobos were gathering it and going into Chicago, where I am sure they got a good price for it. The supervisor reported to law enforcement. Quite a show cutting and burning the weed.

I also learned what it was to pick wild mushrooms and fry them up. Very tasty dish.

Divorced and pretty much homeless, with bills to pay, I moved into the trainman bunkhouse which became my home until I could get on my feet and debt free.

A part-time job delivering furniture for a furniture store in Hammond and working all the overtime I could get with the railroad. I finally I was able to move into my own apartment and become a real person again.

My next part time venture was to become a knife salesman for the Cutco company and, surprisingly enough, I did very well.

I met a lot of people, sold a lot of knives and still use my demonstration set after over 50 years.

Adventures in the Air

With the use of the G.I. Bill 1 decided to learn to fly small fixed wing aircraft, mostly as hobby, but I figured if I got my commercial licenses, it might turn out to be another avenue for a career. The experience was a good one, and I have said many times that the greatest sense of accomplishment was when the trainer pilot got out of the airplane and said take her up as I left the ground realizing it was just me and the birds, what a feeling.

From a Piper J-5 to a Piper J-3, Piper 150, Stinson 150 Cessna 210 I soloed and flew for my own pleasure, but never took the test for private licenses. One of the most exciting things that happened while flying was when a friend of mine who owned a Stinson 150 asked me to fly to Joliet, Illinois with him in the dead of winter. We had flown out of the Griffith, Indiana airport which was a paved runway and on the way to Joliet we saw a couple of small planes sitting in a shed near a homemade runway and my friend said he had often wanted to land there and meet the owner but never had. He asked if I would mind landing there for a visit with him. Of course I liked the idea and down we went for a fly by. Everything looked good so we came back around for a landing. As we hit the grass we realized the ground had been frozen and had just toughed up causing the ground to be soft so we continued up to the top of a slight grade and a terrace before stopping.

Concerned whether we would be able to get airborne we decided to take off if possible. Full throttle only caused us to get a very slow start so I stepped out of the plane and began pushing on the wing strut to help us get going. The extra help got us going fairly good and not being able to run any faster I swung in the plane just as we reached the terrace and the bounce put us airborne.

Back in the air, we realized that the airplane had, what was called wheel pants which covered one half of the wheel and enclosed on each side. They had filled with mud as we took off and due to the air temp had frozen to a solid block leaving us with rubber tire skids to land on. Quickly we decided we would not land on a paved runway and the best thing to do was to contact the Hammond-Chicago airport in Hammond, Indiana where the runways were sod. We did just that and after water being sprayed on the grassy area we were able to land safely. We cleaned out the heel pants and returned to Highland airport.

Another interesting venture was to fly out over Lake Michigan, and Meigs Field bordering the lake near Chicago, which always had a rather heavy cross wind.

As I recall, my flight instructor's name was Bob and he was believed to have logged about 8000 hours in a fighter plane during the second world war, He was quite a daring flier and had complete confidence in the air plane.

One day I was hanging out at the airport and a friend of Bobs came flying in in a vintage biplane and invited Bob to take her up saying that he had just purchased the old girl and she flew like a charm. Naturally, Bob jumped at the offer and turned to me to ask if I would like to take a ride. Sure I said, so I followed him out to the plane where he placed me in the front seat of the open cockpit and he climbed in the rear. Let me tell you I have had some fun and exciting times but this surely was one of the most memorable highlights of my life up to that point.

We taxied out to the runway and faced the slight wind that was blowing where, without hesitation, Bob gave the old bird full throttle and off we went. No sooner had we lifted off the runway, we rolled upside down and fl the pattern that way until we rolled back upright and began a most extraordinary flight over the Indiana countryside. Putting the old open cockpit airplane through its paces, we did it all, barrel rolls, dives, wing overs, spins, free fall, loops and whatever else he knew how to do.

As a student pilot we had restrictions as to where we were allowed to fly and for the most part that was not a problem because we had a rather large area to fly in however lake Michigan was a rather attractive area from the air and I always liked to fly out that way when the instructor was along. One day the weather was nice, and the traffic was light, so I decided I would ease out to the lake area for a look around. As I was flying along the beach, I had not noticed the cloud moving in from the lake and when I decided to make a turn back I went out over the lake. As I turned I entered the cloud and believe me I was completely lost. I had heard the old saying "You can't fly by the seat of your pants" and boy, did I find that out quickly. I managed to set the plane on the proper turn to come back out of the cloud and sure was glad when I could see the lake again. Needless to say I didn't fly back out to the lake solo again.

One day my trainer took us up to 5,000 feet and cut the engine off. The prop stopped and we were powerless. He said "I have it" while putting it in a dive until the prop turned and he started the engine again. A piper J5 was started manually pulling the prop from the ground. We pulled out of the dive and he said they tell you an air start can't be done. I just wondered if it could. Don't ever do it without altitude. As I said he was quite a guy.

After a while I decided that flying was an expense I should not have and due to the fact my wife wouldn't even go to the airport with me much less get into an air plane with me at the stick so I decided not to renew my flying status. I truly did love to fly and still do, although not as a pilot.

Chapter 6

THE LADY THAT ALLOWED ME TO CHANGE MY LIFE

Sometime during my playing the field, I ran into a young lady that changed everything and allowed me to get on the right track toward having a family and career. This girl was about

the prettiest thing I had seen in a while and I was in love again. And this time for good.

I met Samantha (from now on referred to as Sam) at a place that had live country music and dancing. The two things we very much had in common and we have managed to keep the same interest for the last 50+ years.

The girl from Tennessee that put me in a spin became my wife after about a year of dating.

We were married in Crown Point Indiana, by a Justice of the Peace; our honeymoon was quite different than the traditional honeymoon because I owned an old VW bus like the hippies drove. This vehicle was a camper with everything but a bathroom. We decided that a honeymoon in the camper would be nice so off we went to Brown County Indiana to spend a week in the hippie van. The weather was cool, as it was late September.

Our honeymoon was great in that little VW bus camper out in the woods of brown county Indiana. After a week, we started back home to Hammond and about 100 miles from home, the engine gave all it had and a rod came through the block. We ended up in the front yard of a farmer who lived on the road. I am sure, because of our appearance, the farmer was very leery of us until we told him the story of our ventures, after which he agreed to allow us to leave the old bus in the yard until we could return. He also agreed to take us to the bus station so we could catch a bus back to Hammond. Luckily, we had enough money to get the necessary tickets and made it back home to our apartment on Webb St.

Chapter 7

THE BIG STORM

In the winter of 1966/67 I was an employee of the Erie Lackawanna rail road as a signal maintainer and it was my job to take care of the double track territory from Griffith, Indiana to the state line of Illinois just across the little calumet river. I was to maintain all train signals and crossing gates and switch controls with switch tower out of Hammond Yard and draw bridge across Little Calumet River where several train companies crossed the river on our bridge. Included in my territory was the railroad switch yard at fi first street down town Chicago. A snow storm was forecast and sure enough it started rolling in over Lake Michigan. The forecast only called for four inches of snow but they sure underestimated this one. We got the four inches then eight, then ten and by now it was too late to plow the roads. The short story is that we were in Hammond, Indiana and sometimes as snow storms come across the lake, it picks up what is known as the lake effect and dumps heavy snow. Chicago was shut down with nothing moving but trains. Hammond got thirty-two inches of snow and drifts up the second story windows. The Chicago Tribune ran a special paper and called it The Big Snow Storm. Well, since I worked for the railroad and they were the only thing running. I went to work for about seventy five hours straight with a catnap or two. I didn't care if I ever saw another snow flake.

When we married in September of sixty seven, we knew we didn't need another winter like this.

Chapter 8

THE TRAIN WRECK

Shortly after our marriage, I was working in a relay case along the side of the Rail Road when a very unusual thing happened.

I was hit by a train and lived. We lived in a small two-room apartment on Webb St in Hammond with no air conditioning and only a very small fan that we named the gnat, because of its size, to keep us cool. I had taken the line-up of trains by phone (the phones at that time were the old crank phones located in a box along the side of the rail road track.) According to the line up the train that was coming out of the yards would be on the west bound rail headed west. I might note we had no radio or walkie-talkies at that time. But for some reason the rail assignment was changed and the train ended up coming out on the east bound rail headed west.

I knew the train was there, heard the whistle and all, but when I backed up from the relay case I didn't know the train was on my track. With only a glimpse from my left eye I saw the engine and all I could do was jump straight up. The engine struck me on a glance and sent me airborne about twenty two feet landing on my left shoulder and left side of my head. Unconscious for about three hours landed up in the hospital with a broken wrist, head laceration and severe bruising all over. Very lucky to be alive, I woke up to see my beautiful wife stand there pretty much in shock.

I was advised to sue the Rail Road by the union lawyer but in order to do I would need to stay in the area and work for the rail road which I thought would not be good. I was out of work for thirteen weeks because of the cast on my wrist so we decided to do a little traveling.

Memorable trips of our lives

My only visible injury was a broken wrist which didn't keep me from doing anything that was a normal act and 1 was not allowed to go back to work with this situation. With Samantha not working, we decided to take advantage of the opportunity and travel, so off we went to West Virginia to visit sisters and a brother there.

After a short visit with them we took off on a great and memorable trip to Niagara Falls, New York. Being newly wed, Niagara Falls was perfect. We did it all, New York, Canada, Rainbow bridge, Maid of the Mist.

After much deliberation, I returned to work and gave a two week notice; we decided to move to Tennessee for several reasons. One, of course, was family, another was raising a family in the Chicago area was not what we wanted to do. I failed to talk about the biggest reason which was the weather. In 1967, the Hammond Indiana area had a snow storm which delivered about thirty-two inches of snow on the flat ground and drifts were unreal. Working seventy-five hours straight during the snow storm was a money maker but was a very unpleasant event. We decided we both knew living there wouldn't happen.

The building we worked out of on the rail road is what we called the Signal Shack and that is just what it was, a little building just off the tracks at the foot of the little Calumet River draw bridge. This is where we gathered every morning and decided where we needed to go that day. We kept all our fuel for the snow burners. Rainy days were filled with stories about the good old days on the rail road and now I look back and we were living the good old days before the mergers trend and before the federal government destroyed the best, most economical method of transit in the US. This was the beginning of the many destructive moves by the politicians to line their own pockets in the name of progress.

Chapter 9

THE MOVE TO TENNESSEE

Our first big move took place in 1968 when we moved to Huntland, Tennessee. I had a 1953 ford truck and a 1962, 98 Oldsmobile Sedan. I didn't figure Sam could drive from Hammond to Huntland by herself so I loaded everything we owned into the back of the pick-up truck and drove to Tennessee. I then got on a Greyhound bus and went back to drive her down in the car. After a short time, we purchased a mobile home and placed it in the back yard of Sam's mother and dad.

New residents of Tennessee

After much searching, I finally landed a job that was totally out of my character and became a sales person for an insurance field. I was assigned a debit in the mountain area of middle Tennessee which rendered some of the most interesting situations of my twenty-eight years of my career in the business.

The mountain area was known to have its own characteristics, such as a place where wild cat whiskey was made and where people that were not from the mountain were not welcome. A place that was inundated with a degree of racism. I will say a measure of these things existed but while I worked there I was acquainted with a lot of local people and some of the finest, salt of the earth, people I have ever known.

We have several stories that tell a lot about the people and their way of life about things that happened while I worked there. As I remember, I traded cars and went to collect from a lady that had known me for some time and that I had collected from regularly. When I pulled into the yard, there was always somebody there and some children playing in the yard, but today no one was in sight. I pulled up near the house and got out of the car when I saw the kids come out from behind the trees and the lady come out on the porch. I said "I was about to think nobody was home" to which she replied "Didn't know who you were in that strange car". I am sure if it had been someone else, no one would have been home.

Another interesting thing that happened was when I was trying to locate an old policy holder for the first time. I stopped at a house and asked the man that came to the door if he could tell me where a certain person lived and he replied "Don't think I know the man he said". "The man two houses down has been here longer than me and he might be able to help you. "I thanked him and drove down two houses, got out and knocked on the door. The fellow came to the door and asked, "Yep?" I explained that I was looking for this particular person and he said "What do you want with him?"

I answered, "I am the new agent for his insurance company," I said. "And I need to collect from him." His reply was "you have found him. I asked him how long his neighbor had lived up the road and he told me seven years and laughed.

While I worked in that area, I had a sales manager who was a great guy. However, he was rather leery of my driving, and especially on the mountain roads at night.

My mode of transportation at the time was a 1963 VW bug.

In the late 60s recapped tires were used by many people and were used exclusively by me on my VW because the cost of about 12 dollars each was affordable. The recapped tires were mostly reliable and lasted for several thousand miles but occasionally developed an air bubble between the tire and the recap, which naturally caused a bumping sound and vibration as it went round. Knowing what the trouble was, I had no reason to be concerned, as it could hardly cause a blowout or result in an accident caused by it.

When the bubble got too big, I would stop and let the air out with a pocket knife and continue on with my travels until I could get another tire, sometimes being hundreds of miles. After working the mountain for a while I knew the road up and down rather well and 1 knew just how fast I could go and learned that if I kept the right front wheel just off the edge of the pavement on an inside curve, it was somewhat like a trolley car on a track.

I was working in the mountain area of Tennessee one night rather late and had my sales manager with me, as we were returning to the office, we had to come back down the mountain and a bump became apparent as we were swiftly rounding the curves. As usual I wasn't too concerned and keep on coming down the mountain. Arriving at the office I let my sales manager out and went on home, which was about 10 miles or so. As I turned into the driveway, much to my surprise, the right front tire blew out.

A sales meeting was routine every Thursday morning and the subject came up about the sales manager spending time with me, to which he resounded "You haven't lived till you come down the mountain with the Fly in the bug."

This is another very interesting event that occurred while working in the mountain area of Tennessee. I was having a problem with the trans axle in my VW and the word got out that I needed a used one to fix the problem. A man approached me and said for 50 bucks he would drop one off in my yard. After looking into it, I found that he was a part of the car theft ring in the area. I did not go for the deal.

Although the insurance job didn't pay very well, we managed to have what we needed to get by. I spent most of the weekends having to do something to my 1963 Bug it so I could go to work on Monday.

Chapter 10

OUR FIRST BORN

On July 4th, 1969 we were blessed with the birth of our first child. After a long 21 hours in labor our daughter Lori Beth Fly was born, weighing nine pounds ten ounces.

We were still living in the trailer house. With so many of Samantha's family all around much attention was given to the baby.

It is hard for younger folks to realize, but in 1969 nobody had phones they carried with them, as the cell phone was only a dream. I knew that Sam was due to have the baby at any time so I made a list of places I would go on my route and about the time I would be there, so if need be they could call and catch me as I was only several miles from home daily. No instant contact or driving down the road talking to home and no such thing as text.

My mother lived in Monroe North Carolina and we made the trip home two times a year with one being in July. We always had a camper of some sort and included at least a two or three day trip to Myrtle Beach, South Carolina. We stayed in a camp ground and enjoyed the beach time. One night we would treat ourselves to a seafood buffet which, at that time, cost about 6.95 per person. The rest of the time, we ate at the camper to keep the cost down.

Memories of the yearly trips are very good for all of us.

When Lori was five years old we moved to Johnson City, Tennessee.

Chapter 11

OUR SECOND BIG MOVE

Our love for music and dancing was still strong, so it kept Sam and me moving among the people and places that had live music for square dancing. Over the years we went to classes and learned to western square dance and went to many places with the square dance club. When moving to another town, we even helped start and were charter members of a new club called the Celebration Squares. We also took lessons in ballroom dancing.

We had purchased a mobile home also and had set it up on the back side of the lot where Sam's mother and father lived in the old restored school house where she had grown up. The trailer was our home for a few years, during which time I was promoted from salesman to sales manager and we moved our home to Tullahoma TN, which was about twenty-five miles from Huntland.

After a few months I was offered a position in the training department of the company, which I took and went on the road traveling the east Tennessee area recruiting and training sales managers in the sales process of the new products. The company had, at that time, just ventured into the area of multi-line insurance. Health, life, auto, home, and annuity were among the products we offered. I traveled to Johnson City every third week and while I was there we lost Sam's father to a heart attack.

When I took the job as training director, we moved the trailer back to the same place we lived near Sam's parents. We were living there when the death of her father occurred, which allowed her to be near her mother, who was in a wheelchair due to a fall causing an unrepairable broken hip.

During this time, I would leave home on Sunday evening and travel to East Tennessee to return on Friday evening. Not spending a lot of time together was not easy, but a living had to be made.

Assignment was to a district office

In 1974 I was offered a promotion and the assignment was to a district office in Johnson City, Tennessee. This was a two staff office with fourteen sales people and two staff managers. New in district management, in a new area, with all new people, was a stressful challenge.

We had the mobile home pulled to East Tennessee and purchased a house in Johnson City for $55,000 dollars. As most people would, we saw many changes that needed to be made in our new home, which was the beginning of a long journey of buying and remodeling homes while doing all the work ourselves.

During the time we lived in this house. We completely remodeled the basement to make a recreation room, a storage and laundry room, and a guest bedroom. Knowing we were on the lower side of the hill with the basement about two feet below ground level I hadn't figured what might happen in case of a heavy rain. Of course, the previous owner didn't tell me that there was no drain system on the back side of the house. Unfortunately we had not had a hard rain for a long period of time and during that time the basement redo had been complete.

The rains came and we ended up with at least a foot of water over the complete basement. Needless to say, we were all upset, including Lori who was now a little over five years old.

Later on we put the house up for sale and when the agent came out to list and when we got to the basement the first thing Lori said, very enthusiastically, "the water was all the way up to here when it rained".

Nothing like keeping everything out in the open. After the rain I had put in a drain system along the back of the house which fixed the problem. Another interesting event in this house was one day Samantha went down to do the laundry and found a five foot snake skin wrapped around the brace that held up a shelf above the washer. This created quite a stir for a while and we later found out the previous owner had kept a black snake in the attic of the house to keep down mice, etc. We got rid of the snake and he complained that he had given five dollars for that snake.

They say it takes all kinds of people to make the world go round and I have learned that is pretty much the truth.

Chapter 12

MOVE FROM JOHNSON CITY TO SHELBYVILLE

After a while in East Tennessee we felt the need to move back to middle Tennessee to be closer to Sam's family so I checked with my old district manager and found there was an agency open in Shelbyville and decided we would move there for a while until a management opportunity came open In the area, which we did. So we sold the house we had bought and made the move to a rental house in a nice neighborhood in Shelbyville.

Lori, our daughter was now about six years old and started to school in the neighborhood near the house we had rented.

We had some neighbors and some kids the same age of Lori so we made friends really fast and they were the kind of friends that would last a lifetime.

The folks across the street were about the same age we were and the children near Lori's age. Ronnie was a farmer at heart and had for a long time, wanted to buy a farm and move back to the country. One day he said "Ken, there is a farm out toward my old stomping grounds and we should buy it together", Well that was something that I found interesting. Being a country boy myself, we decided to ride out and look at the farm where we found an old farm house in bad repair but livable and so Samantha and I talked it over and decided favorably. We bought the farm as joint owners with the neighbors and decided it with the house place being on our part.

With some clean up and quick repairs we moved in the old farm house.

Needing a complete paint job, and much more but attention had to be turned into more pressing jobs such as installing a wood heating system and addressing the water problem.

This house had a drilled well on the back porch and it turned out to be sulphuric water. Now if you ever had any dealings with sulphuric water you know it has a very unpleasant smell. Kinda like a combination of rotten eggs and rotten cabbage.

It also had a black sediment in it. Someone had installed a salt treatment system which was very outdated and worked poorly. We had to make do with it because at that time there was no city water running out the road we lived on. We made do with this for some years and when the public water system came to our area we were some happy people. Now the house didn't smell like rotting eggs any more.

As I mentioned we had to heat strictly with a wood burning stove which meant the weekends were spent cutting wood for the winter.

Being country folks we had a full garden, chickens, cows, ducks, turkeys, and made use of these things for food.

I have always thought if some else could do something there was no reason why I couldn't do it also.

I recall the kitchen had a very small window in it and Sam always complained about it so I decided to replace it with a bigger one. My mother had come up from North Carolina to visit during the same time I planned to replace the window so I went to town and bought a four foot by four foot solid window for the kitchen.

I think Mom was expecting it to be a big job but my plan was simple. I took the old window out and with my chain saw I cut a four by four hole in the side of the house and installed the new window. I never will forget Mom saying she never saw anything like that before. Many things happened while we lived there. Seemed like one unusual event after another. Our neighbor up the road had a quiet colorful reputation and was a real character.

It seems that he had been drinking and playing cards with a friend when they got into an argument and his friend ended up with a thirty eight bullet in him dead on the spot. Another old man shot himself to death on the road just down from our house.

Chapter 13

THE BIRTH OF OUR SECOND CHILD

Jonathan D Fly was born in August 1979.

Still working on the outside of the old house and traveling to the Columbia area daily I decided to take a few days off when the baby came and work on the window replacement at home while helping Samantha with the baby.

When the time came to pick them up at the hospital I had been having a backache and some pain and figured it was a kidney stone which I had earlier problems with. I arrived at the hospital and the nurse asked "are you OK?" So I told her about the pain.

She said "I don't think we can release the mother and child to you in this condition," so we arranged for me to go to the local doctor. After the exam, the doctor assured me I had a kidney stone and was in for some real pain in the next few hours or maybe days. He gave me Darvon for the pain but said if you are going to drive you can't take this stuff. I assured him I was only going about five miles to home and didn't plan to go anywhere else. They decided it would be OK so off we went with the mother and new baby.

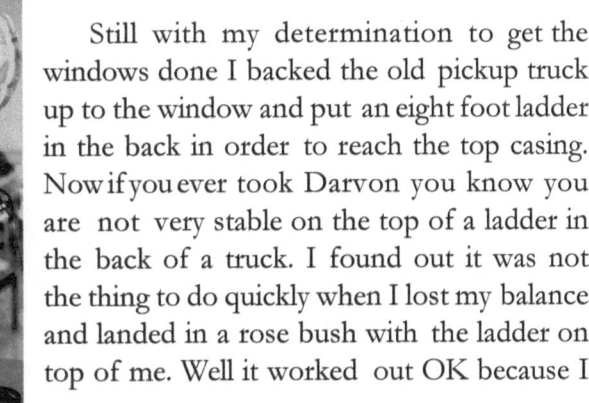

Still with my determination to get the windows done I backed the old pickup truck up to the window and put an eight foot ladder in the back in order to reach the top casing. Now if you ever took Darvon you know you are not very stable on the top of a ladder in the back of a truck. I found out it was not the thing to do quickly when I lost my balance and landed in a rose bush with the ladder on top of me. Well it worked out OK because I went in the bathroom in terrible pain and passed the stone.

Wow, the pain was gone and the rose bush and fall didn't hurt much so back to work with no more Darvon.

All went well and we had Lori, now ten years old, and Jonathan was still a new born. Cows, chickens, ducks, turkeys, dogs and a garden were our pastime as Samantha was not doing public work but had her hands full with all the things going on.

Music and dancing has always been a big part of our lives so the music was going at the house from early morning to late night. As I said earlier I played guitar from an early age following my Dad's lead and had quit while in service but picked up a cheap Harmony flat top guitar while working at the Rail Road for pastime not expecting to do more than that. Lori showed an interest and started guitar lessons weekly.

Being a more reserved person, she was able to learn and play the guitar but never developed a real interest so she stopped taking lessons. Jonathan was a complete other story when it came to music. He entered this world keeping the beat to country music with his hands.

This started us on a long venture involving music.

Chapter 14

SAMANTHA'S TUMOR

Sam had always had a slight under bite and it seem to be getting more prominent as time went by. We had noticed that her ring size was changing and also the size of her hands and her feet were getting larger so she went to the doctor to see about having the under bite fixed and got a real shocker. The doctor sent her for some test and she was diagnosed with a pituitary tumor.

This would have been about 1983 as Jonathan was three years old and at that time things were going pretty well. Things changed rather rapidly as Sam was admitted to Vanderbilt Hospital in Nashville where she stayed for 18 days while the needed surgery was performed. Fortunately the tumor was not malignant but was very extensive. This new procedure had been developed by a doctor at Vanderbilt and we were lucky enough to get the surgeon, Doctor Cully Cobb, who had developed the procedure.

Surgery went well but required twenty five radiation treatments which meant 25 days of additional travel to Nashville which was about one hour and fifteen minutes away.

This meant coordinating work, Lori getting to school and Jonathan taken to a baby sitter daily along with me going to the hospital every day. Somehow with the help of friends we got through the ordeal but it was surely a life experience and caused us all to learn a great deal.

Due to the damage done by the growth caused by the tumor Sam had to have major facial surgery done which was actually worse than the tumor surgery, but of course not as life threatening as it was not dealing with the brain like the other.

With her mouth wired together eating was strictly liquids and weight loss happened and was one of the good things coming from it all. Amazingly enough, being a strong willed and healthy person, Sam held it all together with little drama and life went on.

Again I will say there is nothing like friends during time of trauma and hard to deal with situations, thanks to all.

Chapter 15

MOVE CLOSER TO TULLAHOMA

Living at the farm house was a good life but not the most convenient as I now had to move employment, with the same company, to Tullahoma, Tennessee which was in another direction and Sam said it would be good if we could get closer and that there was a big story and a half house for sale on the Tullahoma highway. A story and a half house was always a favorite for her so we looked at the house and after much consideration we made a deal.

The big problem was we had to sell the farm and got a contract on it but after we had already purchased the big brick house, the deal fell through and the agent had lost the buyer who lived in Florida due to a misunderstanding. Desperate to get rid of the farm in order to pay for the next place I located the prospect and fixed the problem with him, but when the sale was made the agent got his part anyway. Not my first experience with people not doing their job and profiting from it any way and certainly not my last. As time goes by I think it is getting worse.

The farm sold and we were back in the remodeling business again. Everything from repair to brick work to wall paper, moving walls, and lining chimneys had to be done. We loved the old place but taxes and county government was a problem at that time so I was elected the president of the local taxpayer's association and the fight to better the situation was on. This went on for some time and we sold The Shoe Fly. I must tell this story -about the Shoe Fly. I was working in Shelbyville and Samantha was not working public work but wanted to do something rather than stay home, so I was on the lookout for just the right thing while out and about. One day I went into a lady's shoe store to locate a policyholder and in conversation found that the store was a discount store of lady's shoes and that it was for sale.

The lady said the owner really needed to sell and that it would be a good buy for somebody. I contacted the owner and then and there I agreed to buy the business.

When I got home I told Sam that I had purchased her shoe store and that it was a store she had shopped and she liked the idea of having it for her business.

"Fred, Samantha's brother was a great cartoon artist and we came up with the name SHOE FLY. I really don't know who came up with the name but asked Fred to design a logo that would fit in the big sign hanging out front of the building. He did that and it was some kind of creature with eight legs and arms. The creature had a different kind of shoe and or purse on each foot or hand, quite an eye catcher so I got a big ladder and painted the sign well. The store did ok and gave Samantha a full time pastime. After a while it was decided it was not worth the effort and we sold out."

But we were not satisfied with just me working and with Sam being so creative, we opened the Flying Carpet Shop next to the house and dealt in oriental rugs and carpet along with a few other things such as brass ornaments and porch rockers and swings.

Business was good and I specialized in furniture with names and logos of customers engraved in them.

Finally we had enough and had for some time had thought about moving to Moore County, Tennessee which was only a few miles away and was one of the places left that you could do nearly anything you liked without the heavy hand of local government so we purchased a beautiful piece of property which backed up to a thousand acres of game reserve. With property not selling very well then we decided to have an auction and sell the property in two sections with much of our furnishings which were mostly antiques. That is what we did. The auction didn't do too well but we came out of it with a profit and moved on.

Chapter 16

MOVE TO MOORE COUNTY

This time our plan was to build a new home and do the building our selves so in order to have a place to live close by so that we could cut down on travel and could work late and leave everything, we purchased an older used mobile home and placed it next to the new house location. Wow, what a change! Four of us moving from eight rooms, four baths and full basement house to a two bedroom trailor.

Hoping it wouldn't be long we dealt with the situation and went to work building again this time from the ground up. I had drawn the house plans myself so we knew just what we wanted. A salt box was the plan but before long we took off the top story and replaced it with a basement which made more sense due to the lay of the property. Taking a little longer than planned we were really ready to get out of the trailer so we moved in with a lot of the work unfinished, I had decided to hand make all the trim and build the kitchen cabinets myself using oak and poplar wood for the various rooms. After lots of long hours we had a nice house and things were good.

It was now time to sell the mobile home and clean up the yard. With the trailer now gone and sold at a slight profit we continued to improve the place without-buildings etc. Lori was on her way toward marriage. The wedding went off without a hitch and now Jonathan, Sam and I were left in the house.

I think it is time now to regress and fill in the gap left in our music life.

Chapter 17

MUSIC HISTORY

Going back to the fact that Lori was taking music lessons on the guitar and Jonathan came into the world keeping time with hands keeping the beat to music that was a daily part of our lives. Dancing was always a big part of our pastime activity, as Sam and I had met dancing. We country street danced, ball room danced, two step, and western swing. It seemed like when the music started we were dancing. Naturally the kids fell into the groove and developed a love for music and dancing.

When Jonathan was four years old Sam bought a baritone ukulele at a yard sale and brought it home for him. Not knowing anything about that instrument I got a fun with the uke book and followed the instructions to tune and chord it. Although I didn't learn to play the uke Jonathan took hold and learned the chords from the pictures in the book and in no time was keeping rhythm along-side me on the guitar.

When Jonathan was five his uncle gave him an A style mandolin for Christmas and again I was not familiar with the mandolin so once again I got a fun with the mandolin book and once again learned to tune the instrument. Like the uke he found G, C, and D chords and in no time was keeping time alongside me on the guitar. Being a blue grass instrument naturally we gravitated to gatherings of bluegrass musicians and the old mountain music. Singing the old songs came natural and before long he was known around town and playing for the local social clubs, vets and churches.

Lori, now a teenager, and not really interested in the music went along to the festivals and music gatherings. Of course it was because at that time there were several young guys her age playing music and so it wasn't so bad after all.

We spent time going to many contests where Jonathan came home a winner.

Fast forward to age thirteen I was talking to my friend and Grand Ole Opry star Charlie Louvin, He asked had we ever taken Jonathan back stage of the Opry where you had to be at least twelve years old to get in. I said no and Charlie said it's time we did.

Mike Snyder and Jonathan had met some time before and Mike had befriended him because of his music ability.

One Saturday night we met Charlie at the Cracker Barrel restaurant in Nashville and went to the Opry with him. We were sitting on stage and saw that Jonathan had slipped away to somewhere. I found him in Mike Snyder's dressing room and had to ask Mike what it would take to play a little backup fiddle with him on the Opry. Snyder knew he played the mandolin but didn't know he played the fiddle. He said to Jonathan "Bring your fiddle up next Saturday. I want to hear you play". We worked it out to return the next week and as he played a tune for Mike he said "Best I ever heard you playing with me tonight". First time on the Opry was quite an experience for him. He went on to play many places with various people which included return trips to the Opry.

I played guitar for him with his first band at age seven until he was about sixteen. We spent many hours enjoying music together until time for me to step aside to allow him to move on to more progressive music. Of course I kept doing my own thing writing songs and playing country and bluegrass music during which time we recorded two CDs, one single and several originals in the music library of the Production Company 615 Music in Nashville.

Chapter 18

THE MUSIC STORE

I, for some time, had been fed up with the corporate world and had been considering a career change or an early retirement.

With our involvement in music and Jonathan, our son, it high school I looked into the possibilities of a music store in Lynchburg as there had never been one in town so I thought it might work. Jonathan was very involved in playing bluegrass music and was known by almost everybody in the surrounding area. He also liked the idea of working at the music shop. He had been operating a lemonade stand on the square in Lynchburg daily after school for some time.

With such a strong love for music and musical instruments we decide to open a music shop in Lynchburg and Jonathan could operate it after school and on weekends. We had the local dealership for Alvarez, Washburn, and Oscar Schmidt musical instruments.

With a loan from a friend we opened the music store in a small building just off the square in town. We had a jam session every weekend and had pickers from all over come to play music at the little shop.

The shop was filled with anything having to do with music such as books, strings amplifiers, picks etc. while giving lessons on guitar mandolin and fiddle.

After thirty years of dealing with the corporate world in sales, and production contracts as a salesman, a traveling field trainer, and as a district manager I felt I had enough so it was time to move on to another journey as far as work goes.

A man I had become friends with was a very successful businessman and after investigating several options I decided to consult him concerning a future in the food business (his line) and something to build a second retirement on.

Then came the expansion and new business adventure, BBQ.

Chapter 19

UNCLE BUNT STEPHENS DAY

In the year 1998 there was a lot of talk about the possibility of starting an annual bluegrass festival in Lynchburg due to the fact that in the year 1926 a man from Lynchburg by the name of Bunt Stephens had won a fiddle contest sponsored by Mr. Henry Ford. Bunt Stephens "Uncle Bunt Stephens", as he was called, won a trip to Detroit. Mr. Ford gave him $1000 in gold, a Lincoln car worth $5000, and a new suit of clothes.

This event had been pretty much forgotten by 1998, so with a little research we came up with a fantastic news report in the local Bedford county paper, where Uncle Bunt lived at the time.

Being the person that owned a music store in Lynchburg and was playing Bluegrass music a lot I was asked if I could put a festival together. After a lot of thought and a strong desire to promote a festival in Lynchburg I took on the task.

I spent many hours spent gathering information on Bunt Stevens and contacting many bluegrass musicians. I put it all together and collected several thousand dollars in sponsors, such as all the Ford dealers in the area, music stores and business in the surrounding area. Being the first of what was to be an annual event, it was hard to get help doing all the work because it was all volunteer based. Supported by the local chamber of commerce we finally were ready to go with the fest and set the date for a Saturday in September 1999. The State representatives agreed to make Uncle Bunt Stephens Day a part of Tennessee history.

We brought in all the known fiddlers from Tennessee, along with any and all other known bluegrass musicians and arranged a contest of the various instruments for a prize. The winners were all entitled to a cash prize and along with the $1000 prize for first place. Winners for 1 thru 7 places received cash.

The charge for parking and the event was $3.00 for the day.

The crowd was good, the music was good, the food was good, and the weather was good. All in all, it was a great success for the first event of its kind in Lynchburg.

We managed to keep the festival alive for three years with very little help and turned it over to the Chamber of Commerce to build on. Due to the lack of worker support, and the fact that I had given as much as I could, the Chamber dropped the event. I always felt that it could have been one of the best events in Tennessee, but as with every event it takes volunteers.

We published an eighteen page paper "1st Annual Uncle Bunt Stephens Fiddle Day". The paper cost $1.00 and had a coupon for a free fiddle which was given away in a drawing at the end of the day.

My hope was that someday someone would pitch up the event and carry it on but so far that willing person has not showed up.

Chapter 20

THE FIRST FOOD WAGON

We, Samantha and I, decided we could build a food wagon and travel to music events, make music and sell Bar-B-Q and snack foods. This would allow us to enjoy our love for music and food while making enough money to keep us going. Well, we just did that and had a measure of success.

Being a business we had planned to build on I we needed to come up with a name and theme that was eye-catching and recognizably different. With my background of the rail-road I could not dismiss the love for, Samantha came up the name Bar-B-Que Caboose. So the wagon would reflect the theme I built it to look like a caboose (last car on the train). The plan worked well and we worked hard to make it succeed. We found it was not easy to cook, pack, refrigerate, and travel to and from events. Setting up and tearing down was more than we had bargained for and then we decided we would try to find a good location for a more permanent set-up. We had set up in Lynchburg a time or two near the music store and figured Lynchburg would be a great place to expand our presence so we did with the music store holding its own and the food business looking like it had possibilities for providing the necessary income needed I decided it was time to make changes.

Chapter 21

THE SECOND FOOD WAGON

Now off the road with the first little wagon and with more space to sit up I built a second wagon and this time a eight by sixteen foot which could house a complete kitchen and still serve to the outside through a large window. Adjacent to the small music store was a large lot and an old house just off the square in Lynchburg. I leased the house and moved the music store into it and was able to set the new wagon alongside the shop while attaching to the utilities. This worked well.

In the lot on the south side of the house we built a nice stage area where we have live music acts on Thursday, Friday and Saturday nights and a show on Saturday afternoon.

When we needed a place for our guests to eat and enjoy the music, we placed picnic tables in the graveled lot.

The heat and rain seemed to be a constant threat; I bought a twenty by thirty foot tent and put it over the table area. Well, this worked great until we got a big storm which left large trees down on everything and really destroyed the tent idea.

After a battle with the elements we decided it would make sense to move inside, but with not enough room in the house for a music store and a food business I leased a building on the square which turned out to be a smart move.

Chapter 22

THE MOVE INSIDE

The food business was more lucrative than the music store, so it naturally became the main priority for producing income. The sale of the music store ended up being a wash but it did allow us to concentrate our efforts on the BBQ business. Naturally we kept the name and logo which had become known in the area.

Samantha had a brother who was a very good cartoonist. This had been his profession for many years in the Chicago area so I commissioned him to design the Bar-B-Q Caboose logo, which is the same one we have used over the years. Now in the leased building, which had been a gift shop, we arranged the area to serve as a kitchen serving bar. We had booths and tables and a music stage in the front window. This is where we continued our nightly music and the Saturday jam sessions.

Samantha bought me a G scale (a garden scale) electric train which I mounted along the wall from the stage area through the wall to the kitchens while the bands played. we would send cups of lemonade from the kitchen to the pickers. Needing more room as the business grew, I placed a large tent in the back with a new stage from the back door to the alley. It was a great place for food and music.

We had local country and bluegrass bands come in on Friday and Saturday nights for music shows and dinner ~ staying open until nine pm.

While the music store was open we met some interesting people and some professional musicians and entertainers. During this time we had put all we had, both time and money, into the business. But we still needed to increase our income and figure out a way to get away for a break if we could. As luck or fate, we had a friend in the music business who said he had a friend in Savannah, Georgia that I needed to meet and that he thought we would get along well together. With this in mind, Samantha and I decided to take a trip to Savannah and meet this guy, so we did just that. This meeting became a long story and an important part of our lives. Henry, we will call him, was a very sharp business man and what you might say was loaded. After finding out that I had been involved in building and remodeling houses, he made me an offer I couldn't turn down.

He said if you will come down here for a while I will provide you with a place to stay (one of his houses), and pay you well if you will build me a cabin in a place called the Delta Plantation of about thirteen hundred acres on the Savannah River. Well, that sounded good to us, so we loaded up the truck with tools and supplies and headed for Savannah with me driving the truck and Samantha driving the car. We took the car so she would have a way around since she would not be working there.

In order to leave the business, we had to find someone to hold down the fort and run the business while we were gone. We found the perfect person, Candy Richard, and put her to work in charge of the cafe.

We stayed with Henry for about three months and had a great adventure in the Delta. We had wild hogs, eagles, swamp panthers were all there, along with some very colorful people in the area.

We ended up building the cabin and a large barn in the swampy area of the Delta which is still standing today. With the newly made friendship of Henry and his wild and crazy ways, we ended up going back several times to work and enjoy the travel it provided us.

Chapter 23

THE RADIO SHOW

I was at the restaurant one day and met with a couple of guys. One was a rather good country singer and the other guy was good was as an emcee with a good radio voice and the ability to add-lib on commercials and interdictions. For now, we will call them Pete and Paul. The theme of our meeting had to do with the idea of a live radio show they had started only a week or so ago. They were thinking of changing their broadcast and going to another radio station which had better coverage and they were looking for a place to host the show. Well, this was right down my alley, so I made the offer and we made the decision to do the show from the dining room of the Barbeque Caboose restaurant on the square every Saturday morning for one hour. Everything went well for some time, and after a while some conflict came between the two guys and left one in charge. We continued the show every Saturday morning. With Paul as emcee and me as the host. We both had a lot of contacts for musical bands and began having guests on the show. Some of them were very well know, and some were Grand Ole Opry stars.

This business grew steadily. We operated the out of the leased building for about six years, all the while doing radio shows every Saturday morning.

This show continued for twenty years until Covid-19 hit and destroyed the social life of many. We just made plans to start back one Friday night per month with recording artist Brenda Lynn Allen as host.

Chapter 24

A LITTLE TRAVEL WAS GOOD

We have always loved to travel and had done some like Canada, Las Vegas, Chicago, Miami, Key West and several other states but we really found pleasure on the east coast.

We had just moved inside to the leased building on the square and had a friend in Lynchburg that heard out we were going to Hilton Head South Carolina for a few days and he said I have a friend down there you need to meet. After getting the contact information we contacted this friend and in no time he was also our friend. This guy just happened to be a very wealthy person and down to earth as he could be.

While visiting with him he found out that I could do most anything having to do with building and remodeling so he made me an offer to live in one of his houses and do some work for him while having enough time off to enjoy the coastal area.

The first thing he asked me to do was build a cabin in the wetlands near the Savannah River. We hired a young person to work with me with whatever I needed to do, This young man was a very good worker and eager to learn everything from speaking good English to whatever I could teach him having to do with construction. The two of us built a neat cabin on a pond and finished it with beautiful heart pine.

With about fourteen hundred acres to build on he decided he wanted a horse barn near the cabin so we drew the plans and started the barn. Seventy four feet long and forty two feet wide with a full loft we had it finished in six weeks.

Now Samantha was with me during this time and we explored the area from Charleston, South Carolina to Jacksonville, Florida. To the amazement of the family we stayed about four months in that area. She got in a lot of shopping and walking with daily strolls in the delta area. I could tell many interesting stories about this friend in South

Carolina but you might have to know him to get the full effect, besides out of respect for his privacy I probably shouldn't go there.

We ended up going back for as much as two weeks at a time and each time had a great experience. This was a great way to enjoy our semi-retirement and was good for us along with making a life-long friend.

New Location

Not being a fan of building a business in a leased property, I was on the lookout for a building to purchase to ensure a long-lasting business.

Fortunately for me, one of the better locations on the square came up for sale. I was able to close the deal, remodel, purchase a new roof and move the bbq business to the new building, not a new building but new to us.

The shock and uncertainty

The underlying story was that the excitement of getting a new building turned out to be a mixed bag. On Monday September ten, two thousand and one I signed the note to buy the building on the square for our new location. We were all ready to get started with renovation, but the world changed the next morning. 9/11/2001 was all that was on the news. I thought oh no, what have we done? What is going to happen to business? Are we going to be at war? How will the business world survive this event? - with no planes in the air and people completely confused ~ as to what to do. As Allen Jackson wrote, "the world stood still."

Lynchburg, being a mostly tourist town, business was dead in the water but we went ahead with the renovation and move. Already a struggling business with short money flow, this really changed things. For several days the streets were bare and for the next year and a half we kept the struggle alive, but with our eyes on the future and belief that things would be ok we kept sinking what money we had in the business and it paid off.

On with the story

We moved the train and installed the track all the way around the dining room, suspended from the ceiling. a real attraction for the customers. Lanterns? Well again you know the thing about my having worked on the railroad. I ended up with a lantern or two from there and became one of those things I collected. As we traveled around the country if I saw a lantern I didn't have or one that was different, I traded for it and several, not all, ended up hanging around the cafe which enhanced the experience of dining at the cafe. Along with the lanterns I also collected some musical instruments which again went along with the theme of the business and ended up in the cafe.

Another thing that enhanced the cafe was the pictures of musicians and writer/singers that we have known and come in contact with over the years, which were many.

The building we bought on the square had been several different businesses as the picture shows being a service station in the fortys.

It was a lumber company and a gift shop to name a few. With a need for more space, I built a large deck on the back which later got framed and closed in for a party room. a drive through window and smoker room on the side and we restructured the front to look like a restaurant rather than a gift shop.

Chapter 25

MY BUSINESS POLICIES

My business ideas have always been if I could do it myself I would do it. But never do a job that was under your pay grade. In other words, don't do a five dollar an hour job when you can be doing a ten or fifteen dollar an hour job. Hire someone else to do the lesser paid job.

When it comes to money if I needed to borrow money I got it for as long a term as I could and paid it off as soon as I could. If I bought something used, I would get a good deal and when it came time to upgrade, if the item was a good as it was when I bought it I expected to get that same back for it or more than I gave.

Help the people you can help and be a gracious receiver when help is offered.

Try to deal with people for who they really are, not who they think they are, or who they appear to be. There is a big difference most of the time.

When buying I always try to get my money's worth and when I am selling a product I try to give the money's worth. Sometimes this is the eye of the buyer or seller but if everybody is happy with the deal, then it was a good deal. This would mean that from situation to situation you may or may not be happy with the same deal.

Meanwhile back to the cafe

Friday and Saturday evening dinners and music show were a weekly event for us at the cafe for several years. Many hours of musical pleasure was had by our customers and by we, the owners.

We had bluegrass and country bands from all around the area for the Friday and Saturday evening shows.

Folks from Nashville's Grand Ole Opry, The Hee Haw TV show, the Ralph Emery TV show, Opry Land Theme Park, bluegrass bands from Tennessee, Alabama, North Carolina, Ohio, Pennsylvania, Florida, Louisiana, Colorado, Germany, Japan, The Netherlands, The Czech Republic, Canada, and Australia have all graced the stage at the cafe. I am sure I missed some, but you get the idea.

I had always had an interest in writing poetry and had written a few songs. Along the way I was able to record a couple of CDs of some of the songs I had written. I became a member of the Nashville Songwriting Association to expand on my love for writing.

We also joined the R.O.P.E Association. This was a group of retired professional people in the music industry where we would meet and enjoy the fellowship of a lot of great entertainers.

One day Samantha said "you should write a Christmas song." I replied "I have tried to write Christmas music I but can't seem to get the hang of it". She told me that with all the crazy stuff I had written that surely I could write a song along the same lines. So I gave up and answered "I would write about a Christmas witch." I did just that and called it "Sadie, The Christmas Witch" along with a cd and illustrated collaring book to go along with it.

With my interest in writing, I decided to jot down some short stories having to do with my years as a youth growing up on a small farm of about forty acres in North Carolina. After several hours of sitting in front of the TV while Samantha watched a movie that I really wasn't interested in I had written my recollection of the events growing up, where we were and how we did things to get by. In 2014 the book was published covering about the first twenty years of my life. This writing is meant to cover from that point in my life until now.

How the best I ever "ate" came about chap

During the first few years we kept having people say that our food was some of the best they ever ate. I told Samantha that we should put a book out for folks to write comments in but we didn't get around to doing that until one day a man asked me if I was the owner and when

I replied he said "this is the best pulled pork and red beans and rice I ever ate". Naturally I asked him where he was from and to my surprise he said Memphis, Tennessee. Well, as you might know Memphis has had a reputation for great BBQ for years and years.

After his comment I went to the kitchen and cut the top off a pizza box and with a magic marker wrote this is best I ever ate" across the top. I took it to his table and laid it down and he said "I will sign that for sure" and he did. I figured an endorsement of this nature should be on display so I stuck it on the wall. The last account I had we had endorsements from every state in the union and many from foreign countries. Having no place to put them all we started putting them on the ceiling. The ceiling quickly became nearly covered and many were on the walls. Folks are still endorsing our food in the same manner.

Of course Facebook Trip Advisor and some other social media forms are ... this is justification for the name "home of the best I ever ate". How are we going to let this business go?

After nearly twenty years of hard work and investment it seemed to be time to retire again and spend time traveling and just doing the things we wanted to do. The answer to this was to either sell the business or have someone to take it over that would keep the theme and follow the long tested recipes that we had used successfully over the years.

Knowing that person would be hard to find, we found ourselves fortunate to have a family member willing and able to change their life style by moving to Lynchburg and continuing the business in its long tradition of satisfying hungry customers with the same quality food that had earned us the name and reputation of being the "best I ever ate".

That person was Lori, our only daughter, who we knew "would fit in really well where we left off. She and her family had been in Kentucky for seventeen years and was not around to see the business go through the changes necessary to become successful. After our ups and downs, Lori took on the task and fell right in line with the business ideas I had used for many years. It is hard to follow the patterns of the past when you haven't been around during the development and experienced the changes over the years of development. Of course everybody has advice as to the changes they would make although they didn't have any investment.

Everybody knows the old saying "if it ain't broke, don't fix it." This turned out to be a great decision for all concerned and so life goes on.

The last leg has got to be good.

Now it was time to get on with things we wanted to do. Samantha had always had a love for antiques and so we bought another building on the square in Lynchburg that had been everything from a feed store to a gift shop and restaurant. After a total remodeling venture we opened a long awaited antique store and filled it up with treasures from all over.

Chapter 26

THE OLD NEW LOG CABIN

After remodeling was done, and even during the time we were working on the old house on Main Street, Lynchburg, getting it the way we wanted it, we had several ideas about doing something with the back yard. We finally decided to build a cabin on the lower portion (of the property), so I began gathering up the materials needed.

Fortunately Samantha's brother had torn down an old log cabin several years ago and had placed the materials in his back lot, covered with some old tin to keep them from weather and decay. I didn't know about the logs until I contacted him to see if he had anything I could use. He was known to have unusual things (stored) around, that he had collected.

Much to my surprise, he told me about the logs and said he would let me have them for a price. After we removed the tin covering the logs, we found that the elements had taken charge of several of them, but there was still enough to get the cabin started, so we loaded them and hauled them to the back yard.

After counting them and measuring them, I found I only had enough for the front of a one room cabin. Now I had to locate materials from another source. It was my aim to use old, reclaimed wood in the project.

I located an old barn that had been falling down years. Once again, the elements had taken their toll on what logs that were left, but the main problem was that the owner of the barn was known to have turned down others who had tried to buy the logs from him. Determined to secure the logs, if possible, I contacted him in person. I told him I understood he wasn't fond of getting rid of the left overs of the old barn, but that I would very much like to purchase them from him. He asked what I wanted them for, so I told him about my plans to build a cabin in my backyard. Much to everyone's surprise, he said to go ahead and get them, with his blessings, before they completely rotted down. I, with the help of my friend and right hand man, Tommy, loaded the logs and placed them in the desired location of the cabin, with the logs I had gotten from Samantha's brother

On a lot near downtown Lynchburg, there stood an old, unsightly building, which the landowner wanted removed. Tommy said, "If you will pay me to take it down, I will give you all the materials from it." Well, what a deal! We got enough 2 x 8 lumber for all the floor joists, enough barn board for the inside walls, and nearly enough for the roof.

The pole rafters came from an old tobacco barn and the cedar for the floor and ceiling came from a local saw mill.

After about six weeks, working part time, we had the roof on and most of the walls covered, I must say, some of the logs were a task for two older guys, with no equipment to lift them, other than brute strength. Sometimes it was quite the challenge.

We stuffed the cracks between the logs with pieces of chicken wire and filled them with mortar which made a rather tight old/new cabin. Now the one room cabin was ready for use.

Tommy and I had been playing country music for quite some years, so we decided one good use for the newly built cabin would be to have some more of our friends, who were old musicians over to have what we call a jam session. We did just that and enjoyed it so much that we decided to jam one night every week, and we did.

After a few months I ran into an old friend who had an old log corn crib that was rotting down. I ended up with enough logs to add a room onto the cabin which made it the perfect size. Now we had a room to put all the instrument cases in, during the jam session.

A Woven hammock on the back porch turned out to be one of my favorite places.

Advertising in Parades

During our time in the restaurant business we have had several kinds of vehicles for the Christmas parades around the area. For example: the first one was a shell that I built to look like a train caboose. It was just big enough to set over a four wheeler and we entered it in several parades around the area.

Something a little bit bigger would be nice, I thought, so we built a train engine on an old Chevy truck frame that had a good 283 horse power engine in it. This engine was made completely of steel and the front was an operational smoker. Following and connected to the engine, was a ten foot steel wagon to represent a coal car, which would carry several people. Following the coal car was a caboose where the kids could ride. This was a hit at most parades we were in.

Unfortunately, with insurance issues, we had to park the train. No insurance company seemed to have a category that would fit it. We ended up selling the train and it went to New Orleans and appeared in the M (Mardi Gras) Parade.

We had a Lincoln limo that we decorated up and filled with kids for our parade vehicle, once.

One year I rode a Segway with a Merry Christmas sign on it. Another time we had Sadie the Christmas Witch in a parade. Guess I just liked to have something different.

Chapter 27

THEN ALONG CAME COVID-19

Well, it seems to never stop in business and turns into a treadmill that you can't get off of without some difficulty so life goes on.

I must add this to writing the latest stump in the road, so to speak. Covid-19 is called among other names, such as, Chinese plague, came to us early in 2019, and as did most businesses, shut the Cafe down for a couple of weeks. Having the only drive-thru window in Lynchburg we decided to keep that part of the business open in order to keep the bills paid and allow some of the employees to keep their job.

We made it thru the worst part of the world shutdown. Before long we were open on a limited bases to maintain the social distancing rule and out came the mask.

In August, Samantha and I were tested for Covid and Samantha was positive so staying home was the only choice. Fortunately, Samantha didn't have a bad case of the virus and was down a couple of days. Then it was my turn so my test was positive now and my experience was a little more severe and after three days in bed I decided if I didn't get up, I was headed for a not good ending. Since I had been planning to build a deck in the back yard, I would go outside to see what I could do. Well, I found that for a few minutes at the time I could drag the lumber in place for the new deck, the few minutes I speak of turned out to be five or ten. After a rest I would get up and try again.

Well, it took some time but with the fresh air and exercise I had built a twenty six by twenty one foot deck. Of course I had to do it all without help because I had the virus. Thankful it turned out the way it did because I feel that is why I made it thru the illness. Also thankful to be in Tennessee where the state government allowed us to decide our own fate rather than a long shutdown as did several other states. Said enough because we are about to get into politics. I | could write a book on the way I feel on that subject. For now, I will let it go.

Chapter 28

STILL UP TO A CHALLENGE

Sometimes life does not go as planned and, a person finds him or herself having to review a situation and pick up the challenge again.

As things go I have taken charge of the BBQ Caboose Cafe again for a restructuring. We will now have a business manager and a kitchen (food) manager.

It was my plan to retire to building things, fish, run my bull dozer and other fun stuff but sometimes things just don't work the way you planned.

My other option would be to sell. At age 80, no problem, I can step up and handle the job.

As I may have said before I have been asked when I would consider my age and Stop all this activity. My answer was "Three Days Before the Funeral". This now includes the title to one of my new songs.

Don't know if I will have time to write the third addition to my Patches of My Life

With my bull dozer, dump truck, wood working shop and my fishing boat, Saturday morning radio show life is good. I just wrote a song with the title, "Three Days Before the Funeral is my Plan." That has to do with the question I have been asked, "when are you going to stop all this crazy running round?"

It has been a good ride and it's still kicking. Maybe not long enough to write a follow up book three, but who knows?????

Summary

- As I look back over my eighty years I have surely been blessed.
- Grew up in a loving family with a good Mother, Dad, Sisters and Brothers with no history of unlawful acts.
- Grew up on a farm learning that side of the tough life. Graduated from high school.
- Became an electrician.
- Served in the U.S. ARMY and was honorably discharged with no disabilities.
- Worked on the railroad and lived in the Chicago area long enough to know that was where I wanted to be.
- Met A beautiful lady from Tennessee and followed her to what I feel is the greatest place to live and have a family.
- Blessed with two children: one boy, one girl, one son in law, and one daughter in law.
- And five grandchildren.
- I have had the pleasure of flying as a passenger and a pilot.
- Have owned big motorcycles, and small motorcycles, big trucks and small trucks, Small boats and a houseboat. Camping trailers and a motor home. Big cars and little cars.
- I have traveled overseas and all over the United States.
- I have played music, written music, and recorded music.
- I have opened and operated multiple businesses.
- So what do I say to all this. I have done a lot of things, some well, some not so well. I have a lot of friends and I guess some enemies. So far, it's been a good ride and I am looking forward to riding on

for a while. I hope you enjoy my stories which are all true. No fiction.

For copies of my music, recordings, and books, you can contact me at the BBQ Caboose Café on the square in PO Box 139, Lynchburg, Tennessee, 37352.

Thank you to everyone for your support!

A little about the music

Like a lot of people I have been asked who was my music influences along the way

"And to this I would have to say many. I have always had a love for music of many kinds, although I never had the opportunity to follow the music business professionally it has always been a big part of my life. As far back as I can remember."

I remember when Dad would play guitar and my sisters would sing while sitting on the back porch. Dad also played the French harp.

Learning the guitar at an early age was very limited and as I grew older and went to public work I spent a little time every payday at the local record shop and came home with a new record of people like Chet Atkins, Duane Eddy, Bill Black, and others."

"Over the last forty plus year I have had many friends like Charlie Louvin, Jim Ed Brown, Jimmy Dickens Bill Monroe and others that have kept my music interest very much alive . As a writer

I have registered with BMI, mostly ballads, I have music in the 615, the Music library and Warner Chapel".

I have added 30 plus songs to this book some of which I have recorded on CDs, some are on YouTube including "DON'T LIVE YOUR LIFE WITH THE BRAKES ON" recorded this year by my friend and recording artist, Brenda Lynn Allen.

All songs written by Ken Fly, BMI. All rights reserved.

Some friends along the way

Index of Songs

THE LEGEND	74
THE DANCE FLOOR	76
TEARS ON MY GUITAR STRINGS	78
TAKE ME BACK TO NASHVILLE	79
RIDING HIGH	81
PRESCRIPTION	83
PARTIAL TO A COWBOY	85
COLOR OF THE WINE	87
MEXICO NO MORE	89
MAMA FOUND A DOLLAR	91
SADIE THE CHRISTMAS WITCH	94
THE MAN MY DOG THINKS I AM	96
DIGGING IN THE DUMPSTER	97
DON'T GET NEAR MY FIRE	99
OLD MAN'S GUITAR RECITATION	100
TWO FINGERS	102
DON'T LIVE YOUR LIFE WITH THE BRAKES ON	104
DON'T WALK ALONE	106
GIRL WITH GOLD IN HER HAIR	108
GUNS GUITARS AND GIRLS	110
JUST AN OLD GUITAR	112
I MET AN OLD COW-HAND	114
YOU LEFT YOUR RING ON MY TABLE LAST NIGHT	116
JUST RETURNED FROM A BATTLE	118
IF YOU KNOW JACK	120
OLD WESTERN COWBOY	122
SUNSHINE	124
HONEY YOU CAN BEAT THAT	126
ROUTE 55 BLUES	128
I-PHONE BLUES	130
LEGEND OF A LITTLE MAN	133
WE WILL DANCE	135

COLORADO BLUE 138
SMELL OF WHISKEY 141

THE LEGEND

D   G   D
ONLY A LEGEND COULD BE KNOWN LIKE THIS
                   A   D
THE WHOLE WORLD KNOWS WHO THIS MAN IS
         G   D
ONLY A LEGEND, COULD BE KNOWN LIKE THIS
                A   D
IN THE HEARTS OF MAN, HIS MUSIC STILL LIVES

TEMP CHANGE:

D   G   D
I KNOW A STORY ABOUT A MAN
           A   D
FOR YEARS HE TOURED ACROSS THE LAND
    G   D
HE WAS KNOWN AS A GENTLE MAN
      A   G
SANG A SONG ALL COULD UNDERSTAND
D   G   D
THE STORY GOES HE WAS DRESSED IN BLACK
             A   D
WENT DOWN SOME ROADS NEVER TO GO BACK
      G   D
STANDING TALL BY THE RAILROAD TRACK
     A   G
WITH THAT GUITAR STRAPPED ON HIS BACK

CH==

HE WALKED THE LINE HE ROAD THAT TRAIN
SOMETIMES DRUGS WORKED ON HIS BRAIN
WENT DOWN TO JACKSON WITH HIS LOVELY WIFE
WORKED UP IN DETROIT ONE PIECE AT A TIME
FOLSOM PRISON NASHVILLE TOO
GREW UP HARD WITH A NAME LIKE SUE
JUST LIKE BROTHERS CHRIS AND WILLIE SAY
ALONG WITH WAYLON COULDN'T STAY AWAY
THAT FINAL STATEMENT IN THE LAST DAYS
HE MADE PROFOUNDLY (I HURT MYSELF TODAY)

THE DANCE FLOOR

```
C                                          G7
OH THE PLACE IS NOT SO CROWDED AFTER ALL
                                    C
THE MUSIC CRISP AND COUNTRY WALL TO WALL
                              F
THE DANCE FLOOR IS NOT SO BIG NOT SO BIG AT ALL
         C                G7             C
AND IF WE'D JUST DANCE I'M SURE WE'D HAVE A BALL

C
IT HASN'T BEEN SO LONG
G7
NOT SO LONG AT ALL

40 YEARS HAS PASSED SO FAST
            C
I HARDLY NOTICED IT WAS GONE

WE HAVE DANCED THE TIME AWAY
      F
AND YES WE'VE DANCED IT ALL
         C          G7     C
BUT IT HASN'T BEEN SO LONG  AT ALL

CH
WE WILL TAKE OUR SEATS AS WE SIT ALONG THE  WALL
THE YOUNG FOLKS MOVE SO FAST ALL AROUND THE  HALL
SURE WE COULD GET OUT THERE AND DANCE
```

DANCE AND SHOW THEM ALL

BUT FOR NOW WE'LL KEEP OUR SEATS ALONG THE WALL

LOOK THEY'RE GONE THERE'S ONLY TWO LEFT ON THE FLOOR

THE MAN JUST PUT THE CLOSED SIGN ON THE DOOR IT'S TIME WE GOT OUR COURAGE UP ONCE MORE

AND TOOK OUR TURN OUT THERE ON THAT DANCE FLOOR

IT'S TIME WE GOT OUR COURAGE UP ONCE MORE AND TOOK OUR TURN OUT THERE ON THAT OLD DANCE FLOOR

TEARS ON MY GUITAR STRINGS

D   A
THERE'LL BE TEARS ON MY GUITAR STRINGS TONIGHT

      A   D D7
THERE'LL BE TEARS ON MY GUITAR STRINGS TONIGHT

    G
WE WILL PLAY SOME HAPPY TUNES

    D
HAPPY SOUNDS WILL FILL THE ROOM

            A   D
BUT THERE'LL BE TEARS ON MY GUITAR STRINGS TONIGHT

IT'S JUST A HAND-ME-DOWN, BUT ITS REALLY BEEN AROUND

PLAYED MANY HAPPY SONGS ALONG THE WAY

THE SONGS I WROTE TODAY I'LL SING WITH ALL MY MIGHT

BUT THERE WILL BE TEARS ON MY GUITAR STRINGS TONIGHT

AFTER ALL THESE YEARS TOGETHER AND THE STORMS WE HAD TO WEATHER

WITH A LOVE SO STRONG FOR ALL THE WORLD TO SEE

THIS WILL ALL END SO FAST THE FUTURE OUT OF SIGHT

AND THERE WILL BE TEARS ON MY GUITAR STRINGS TONIGHT

TAKE ME BACK TO NASHVILLE

C
G   **C**
TAKE ME BACK TO NASHVILLE TO OLD COUNTRY
G   **D**
TAKE ME BACK TO NASHVILLE THE WAY IT USED TO BE
G   **C**
TAKE ME BACK TO NASHVILLE TO THE RYMON
G   **D**   **G**
TAKE ME BACK TO NASHVILLE'S GRAND OLE OPRY

G
WELL EVERY THING HAS CHANGED NOW
C
COUNTRY IS NOT WHAT IT USED TO BE
G
SOME SAY IT MAKES NO DIFFERENCE
                      D
BUT IT'S A SAD SOUR NOTE TO ME
G
SOME THINGS ARE BETTER OFF LEFT ALONE
    C
AND NOW I BELIEVE IN THAT
G
COUNTRY IS GREAT JUST LIKE IT IS
D   **G**
SO LET'S JUST LEAVE IT AT THAT

G
THOSE OLD SONGS THAT HANK WROTE
C
CHARLIE AND IRA TOO
G
THEY WILL BE AROUND WHEN THE NEW STUFF IS GONE
                                          D
AND THE FLASH IN THE PAN IS THRU
G
YOU SEE THEY'VE STOOD THE TEST OF TIME
C
WRITTEN AND SUNG TRUE TO FORM
G
SO SING ME A GOOD OLD COUNTRY SONG
                            D
WHERE COUNTRY MUSIC WAS BORN

TAKE ME BACK TO NASHVILLE TO OLD COUNTRY
TAKE ME BACK TO NASHVILLE THE WAY IT USED TO BE
TAKE ME BACK TO NASHVILLE TO THE RYMAN
TAKE ME BACK TO NASHVILLE'S GRAND OLE OPRY
TAKE ME BACK TO NASHVILLE'S GRAN OLE OPRY

RIDING HIGH

G
RIDING HIGH

G
RIDING HIGH

G
RIDING HIGH

G   **C**
RIDING HIGH WEST OF THE PECOS

G   **D**
UNDER THE CLEAR BLUE SKY

G   **C**
SAND, CATUS AND BARE GRASS ARE DRYING

      G   **D**   **G**
AS THE DESERT SUN RISES HIGH

G   **C**
CATTLE ARE SLOWING SOUTH TOWARD DELRIO

G   **D**
MARRIAGES ON THE HORIZON ARE SEEN

G   **C**
CAREFULLY PICKING STEPS THROUGH THE BASON

      G   **D**   **G**
AS THE THORNS AND RATTLERS SO MEAN

G   **C**
WELCOME THE COOLING AND BEAUTY OF SUNSET

G   **D**
THE SMOKE AND THE CHUCK WAGON SMELL
G   **C**
IT'S UP ON THE TRAIL AGAIN BY SUNRISE
G   **D**   **G**
PUSHING CATTLE TEN MILES WE'LL DO WELL

CH==

NONE CAN ECHO THE FEELING OF A COWBOY
AS HE'S WILD AND FREE AS THE BREEZE
STRADDLE THE LEATHER TOP OF A STALLION
IN THE DISTANCE THE TRAILS END A TEASE
THE MADAMS' GIRLS WAITING IN COW TOWN
POCKETS JINGLE AT THE END OF THE TRAIL
THUS IS THE GLAMOROUS LIFE OF A DROVER
THE LIFE THE FREE KNOW SO WELL

PRESCRIPTION

G
FEELING KINDA POORLY THE OTHER DAY
G
WENT TO SEE OLD DOC HERE'S WHAT HE HAD TO SAY
G
TAKE THIS PRESCRIPTION HOME TO MAMA RIGHT NOW
G
GET IT FILLED IF YOU FIGURE OUT HOW
G
TOOK ONE LOOK KNEW IT WOULDN'T WORK
G
THE LOOK ON MAMMA'S FACE WOULD BE A GREAT BIG SMERK
G
STUCK IT IN MY POCKET GAVE A BIG OLD BOW
G
LIKE TO GET IT DONE WITHOUT A PROBLEM PAL
C
MAMMA IS NOT THE KIND TO BE SUCKERED IN
G
TO DO A BUNCH OF STUFF LIKE A MOTHER HEN
    D
IT MIGHT JUST HELP TO TELL HER WHERE I'VE BEEN
                                                    G
TO SEE OLD DR HOLLINS WITH HIS SNEAKY GRIN

G

HERE'S WHAT IT SAID

G

BREAKFAST IN BED EACH AND EVERY DAY

G

THREE BACK RUBS DONE THE RIGHT WAY

C

A TLC AND A PRN

G

BEST IDEA SINCE I DON'T KNOW

D

YES SIR DOCTOR I'LL SAY IT AGAIN

G

BEST IDEA SINCE I DON'T KNOW WHEN

MAMA GAVE ME THAT LOOK AND SAID
WHAT DOES THIS MEAN
ARE YOU REALLY SICK OR IS THIS A SMOKE SCREEN
WHAT KIND OF DR IS THIS GUY
COULDN'T FILL THIS ORDER EVEN IF I TRIED
YOU BOTH MUST BE CRAZY IF YOU THINK I CAN
CAN'T TAKE ORDERS FROM A CRAZY MAN
HERE'S WHAT IT SAID
BREAKFAST IN BED EACH AND EVERY DAY
THREE BACK RUBS DONE THE RIGHT WAY
A TLC AND A PRN
BEST IDEA SNICE I DON'T KNOW
YES SIR DR I'LL SAY IT AGAIN
BEST IDEA SINCE I DON'T KNOW WHEN

PARTIAL TO A COWBOY

CH===

G   Em
I'M PARTIAL TO A COWBOY.
G   Em
THAT'S WHAT I HEARD HER SAY.
G   Em   C
I'VE ALWAYS DREAMED OF GOING TO A COWBOYS
D   G
HIDE-A-WAY
G   Em G   Em G
WATCH THAT BIG OLD SUN SINKING IN THE WEST HEAR.
                              Em   C
HEAR THOSE COWBOYS HOWLING AS WE LAY
D   G
DOWN TO REST

C   G   C
STANDING BY THE DOORWAY HIS FOOT AGAINST THE
G
WALL
C   G   A   D
DRESSED IN HIS COWBOY GET-UP HATS JEANS AND ALL
    C   G   C
SHE TOOK HIM BY THE HAND LED HIM THROUGH THE
G
DOOR

C   G   D
DETERMINED TO HAVE HIM FIRST OUT ON THAT OLD
G
DANCE FLOOR

CH===

C   G   C   G
NOW THE DANCE IS OVER THE MOON IS SINKING FAST
C   G   D
ALL THE THINGS SHE DREAMED ABOUT WAS COMING
          G
TRUE AT LAST

G   Em   G
I'M PARTIAL TO A COWBOY. THAT'S WHAT I HEARD HER
Em
SAY
G   C   D   G
COMING TO A CLOSE WAS A COWBOYS' PERFECT DAY

COLOR OF THE WINE

```
C                       F            C
LOOK AT THE GLASS AND THE COLOR OF THE WINE
I SEE YOUR REFLECTION IN THE ROUND GLASS NEXT
     G7
TO MINE
         C
WE ARE NOT SHOULDER TO SHOULDER THOUGH I
F           C
WISH IT COULD BE TRUE

F           C              G7
I WISH THIS WERE A MIRROW AND THE WHOLE WIDE
C
WORLD COULD KNOW

         F                      C
YOU'RE SITTING THERE WITH HIM SHE'S HERE
BECAUSE SHE'S MINE
           A
WE ARE LOOKING AT EACH OTHER THROUGH THE
G
WARM GLOW OF THE WINE
           G                          F
THEY KNOW NOT OF OUR FEELINGS OR THE PLACES
           G
THAT WE GO
```

```
      F                    C
THE TIME WE SPEND TOGETHER IN OUR SECRET
        C
RENDEZVOUS

  F                        C
LOOK AT THE GLASS AND THE COLOR OF THE WINE

WE ARE LOOKING AT EACH OTHER
                G
THROUGH THE WARM GLOW OF THE WINE
C
WE'RE NOT SHOULDER TO SHOULDER THOUGH I
  F            C
WISH IT COULD BE TRUE
   F             C
I WISH THIS WERE A MIRROW AND THE WHOLE WIDE
D          C
WORLD COULD KNOW
```

YOU'RE SITTING THERE WITH HIM SHE'S HERE
BECAUSE SHE'S MINE
WE'RE LOOKING AT EACH OTHER THROUGH
THE WARM GLOW OF THE WINE
THEY KNOW NOT OF OUR FEELINGS OR THE PLACES
THAT WE GO
THE TIME WE SPEND TOGETHER IN OUR SECRET
RENDEZVOUS

MEXICO NO MORE

C   G
I AIN'T GOING TO MEXICO NO MORE
                            G
I AIN'T GOING TO MEXICO NO MORE
F
FROM BROWNSVILLE TO EL PASO
      C
THE BORDER IS IN A WAR
                 G   C
AND I AIN'T GONG TO MEXICO NO MORE

C   G   C
GUNFIRE ACROSS THE RIVER SOUNDING LOUD
DEALERS OF THE DRUGS RUNNING THROUGH THE
G
CROWD
F   C
YOU'RE NOT SAFE IN ANY OF THE STORES
                 G   C
SO I AIN'T GOING TO MEXICO NO MORE

CH==

CRUISE BOATS ARE CLOSING UP THEIR PORTS
ALL THE LOW PRICED SHOPPING SOON TO BE NO MORE
DRUG CARTEL CAUSING QUITE A ROAR
NO I AIN'T GOING TO MEXICO NO MORE

ALL THAT NATURAL BEAUTY GOING TO WASTE
POWER AND CONTROL BY THE HUMAN RACE
WE SEE AND HEAR THE MADNESS
WHAT ELSE MIGHT BE IN STORE
DON'T KNOW BUT I AIN'T GOING TO MEXICO NO MORE

MAMA FOUND A DOLLAR

G   C
DECEMBER OF 1942 THINGS WERE KIND OF TOUGH
G   D
REGARDLESS OF THE STRUGGLE INCOME NOT
ENOUGH
G   C
TO FURNISH GIFTS FOR ALL THE KIDS CHRISTMAS
NOW IN SIGHT
G   D
DISAPPOINTMENT WOULD BE HERE TO FACE ON
G
CHRISTMAS NIGHT
G   C
THAT OLD VICTROLA HORN LIKE A FLOWER ON A
STAND
      G   D
WHERE MOM WOULD HIDE A DOLLAR SO LATER SHE
COULD SPEND
G   C
SHE HAD CHECKED THAT OLD HORN MANY TIMES
THIS YEAR
          G
SHE WOULD SHAKE IT JUST ONCE MORE FOR
C   G
CHRISTMAS TIME WAS HERE

SHE KNEW THERE WAS NOTHING THERE AS SHE
TURNED IT UPSIDE DOWN
SOMETHING FELL TO THE TABLE CRUMPLED WITHOUT
A SOUND
JOY NOW OVER TOOK HER AS SHE SANK INTO A CHAIR
HAPPY KIDS AT CHRISTMAS AFTER ALL THE ANSWER
TO HER PRAYER

C   G
MAMA FOUND A DOLLAR IN THAT OLD VICTROLA HORN
ONE DOLLAR THOUGHT NOT VERY MUCH ITS'
      D
CORNERS FRAYED AND TORN
  G   C
LIKE MANNA FROM UP ABOVE IT FELL FROM THAT OLD
HORN
     G   D
SHE WOULD SHARE IT WITH A NEIGHBOR ON THIS
    G
CHRISTMAS MORN

G
FRUITS AND NUTS IS ALL IT BOUGHT BUT
OH WHAT A CHRISTMAS TREAT
GIFTS WERE NON EXISTENT THOUGH
WE HAD FOOD TO EAT
THE CHARING OF A DOLLAR IS ALL IT TOOK THAT YEAR
TO FILL TWO HOMES WITH SMILES AND LOVING
CHRISTMAS CHEER

NEIGHBOR BEING NEIGHBOR ON THIS CHRISTMAS MORN
NEIGHBOR SHARING CHRISTMAS ON THIS DECEMBER MORN
G

SADIE THE CHRISTMAS WITCH

A
SADIE THE CHRISTMAS WITCH ITS EVE WHEN
SHE COMES BY
E
RIDING ON HER CHRISTMAS TREE LIGHTING
UP THE SKY
A
SHE HOLDS OUT HER MAGIC WAND WATCH
THE STARDUST RISE
E   **A**
SADIE THE CHRISTMAS WITCH LIGHTING UP THE SKY
SHE'S NOT LIKE CINDERELLA'S WITCH OR DOROTHY'S
FROM THE WEST
SHE HAS A PLAN OF ACTION FAR BETTER THAN THE REST
SHE DARTS AROUND ON CHRISTMAS EVE
HER LIGHTS ARE SHINING BRIGHT
FOLLOWING THE JOLLY MAN HER TRIO
WILL LAST ALL NIGHT
A
NOW IF YOU HAVE TOLD OLD SANTA OF YOUR
CHRISTMAS LIST LAST YEAR
E
THEN ON CHRISTMAS MORN YOU HELD BACK A TEAR
A
BECAUSE HE DID NOT BRING IT AND DROP IT FROM ALOFT

I REALLY THINK IT DID AND SADIE HAULED IT OFF
SADIE THE CHRISTMAS WITCH ITS EVE
WHEN SHE COMES BY

CH:

A
WHY DID SHE DO IT TAKE AWAY YOUR GIFT
E
SHE DID IT TO HAIL SOMEONE WHO NEEDED A
CHRISTMAS GIFT
A
SHE GAVE IT TO ANOTHER ONE JUST DOING
SOMETHING GOOD
E
YOU SEE SADIE THE CHRISTMAS WITCH
IS A CHRISTMAS ROBINHOOD

THE MAN MY DOG THINKS I AM

MAN'S BEST FRIEND AS WE ALL KNOW
LOVES TO FOLLOW YOU WHERE WE MIGHT GO
NOT HUMAN THOUGH TO US SOMETIMES MAY SEEMS

IT MAKES NO DIFFERENCE HOW YOU LOOK
WHETHER YOU'RE A SAINT OR YOU'RE A CROOK
THEY THINK YOU'RE THE GREATEST THING ON EARTH
THEY RESPOND TO YOUR COMMAND
WHETHER IT BE VOICE OR BY YOUR HAND
THEY DO WHAT YOU REQUEST WITHOUT REGRET

THEY FEEL FOR YOU WHILE YOU'RE IN PAIN
BY YOUR SIDE THEY WILL REMAIN
PROTECT YOU WHEN THERE'S DANGER OR A THREAT

WE GO THROUGH LIFE WITH ITS UPS AND DOWNS
UNCERTAIN EACH TIME WE TURN AROUND
TRYING TO FIGURE OUT THE BEST WE CAN
WE COULD TAKE A LESSON FROM OUR PET
TURNS OUT THEY'RE OUR BEST FRIEND YET
I'D DO WELL TO BE THE MAN MY DOG THINKS I AM

I'D DO WELL TO BE THAT MAN THAT MY DOG THINKS I AM
NO MATTER OF THE WEATHER
WE ALWAYS STICK TOGETHER
BY MY SIDE HE WILL STAND
I'D DO WELL TO BE THE MAN
THAT MY DOG THINKS I AM

DIGGING IN THE DUMPSTER

CH== D-G-D-E-A. D-G-D-A-D

DIGGING IN THE DUMPSTER DIGGING IN THE DUMPSTER
DIGGING IN THE DUMPSTER TO SEE WHAT I CAN FIND
THEM RICH AND FANCY PEOPLE COULD KICK MY BEHIND
CAUSE I'M DIGGING IN THE DUMPSTER TO SEE
WHAT I CAN FIND
I SAW A MAN STANDING

IN A DUMPSTER ONE COOL DAY
I ASKED HIM WHAT HE WAS DOING
EXPLAINED IT JUST THIS WAY
I'M DIGGING IN THE DUMPSTER
TO SEE WHAT I CAN FIND
I'LL TAKE IT HOME AND CLEAN IT UP
AND THEN IT IS ALL MINE
HAVE YOU EVER LOST A PARING KNIFE
OR A BRAND NEW DIAMOND RING
A PRICELESS PIECE OF SILVER
OR SOME OTHER VALUED THING
YOU LOOKED AND LOOKED AROUND
AND WONDERED WHERE IT WENT
THIS GARBAGE PICKER FOUND IT
AND SOLD IT FOR A MINT

CH==

DID YOU EVER SEE SOMETHING

AT A DUMPSTER WHEN YOU PASSED
BUT FOR THE FEAR OF BEING SEEN
YOUR FOOT STAYED ON THE GAS
WELL I DON'T HAVE THAT PROBLEM
THE FEAR OF BEING SEEN
I'LL JUMP INTO A DUMPSTER
ANY OLD TIME I PLEASE

NOW ALL THAT GOOD AND PRETTY STUFF
YOU HARDLY CAN BELIEVE
THAT HAS BEEN THROWN AWAY
IS MINE ALONE TO KEEP
SO DON'T SPEND YOUR TIME
FEELING SORRY FOR ME
I'M DOING WHAT I WANT TO DO
AND ALL MY STUFF IS FREE

DON'T GET NEAR MY FIRE

A

BY CANDLELIGHT I SEE YOU	C
HOW MY POOR HEART DOES YEARN	F
BUT DARLING DON'T GET NEAR MY FIRE	FC
YOU SURELY WILL GET BURNED	G7 C

I LONG FOR OUR RELATIONSHIP	C
TO LAST A LIFETIME DEAR	F
BUT THAT UNEASY FEELING STARTS	FC
EACH TIME THAT YOU DRAW NEAR	DG

DON'T BE FOOLED BY DREAMS	C
FORTUNE OR FAME	
OR WORDS THAT YOU MIGHT HEAR	F
IT'S ALL JUST LIKE A VAPOR AS IT RISES	
IN THE AIR	FCGC

BK

IT'S NOT WHAT YOU ARE FEELING
AS LIFE'S PAGES YOU TURN
DARLING DON'T GET NEAR MY FIRE
FOR YOU SURELY SURELY WILL GET RETURNED

BY CANDLELIGHT I SEE YOU
HOW MY POOR HEART DOES YEARN
BUT DARLING DON'T GET MY FIRE
YOU SURELY WILL GET BURNED

OLD MAN'S GUITAR RECITATION

WENT TO WORK ON A RIVER BOAT IN THE YEAR OF 2010
PLAYING MY GUITAR LIKE I COULD PLAY BACK THEN
RIGHT IN THE MIDDLE OF LIBERTY THIS OLD MAN
WALKED IN
HE SAID WHERE DID YOU LEARN TO PLAY LIKE THAT,
AND WHERE THE HECK YOU BEEN

I THOUGHT I'D SEE THAT OLD MAN BUT
COULDN'T REMEMBER WHEN
HE TOOK MY OLD GUITAR LAID IT ON HIS KNEE AND THEN
AND I HEARD THINGS THAT NIGHT I'D NEVER HEARD AGAIN
I SAID TO WHAT'S YOUR NAME OLD MAN AND WHERE
THE HECK YOU BEEN
A PAWN SHOP IN NASHVILLE WHERE THIS ALL BEGAN
I PICKED UP THIS OLD GUITAR DIDN'T LOOK LIKE MUCH
JUST THEN
PICKING CAME SO EASY THE NECK AND SOUND SO FINE
MY FINGERS MOVING ACROSS THE STRING LIKE THEY
WERE NOT EVEN MINE
I DRAGGED THIS OLD GUITAR EVERY WHERE I WENT TO
JUST COULDN'T LAY IT DOWN, WORTH THE HUNDRED
I HAD SPENT
NOW IT SEEMS TO BE AT HOME ON THE OLD MAN'S KNEE
FUNNY HOW HE SEEMS TO PLAY SOME NOTES
JUST LIKE ME

I WOULD SAY HIS FINGER STYLE THE BEST I EVER SEEN

MY HOW THAT OLD MAN COULD MAKE THAT GUITAR RING

I SAID PLAY ME ANOTHER TUNE LET'S SEE IF YOU CAN SING

HE HANDED ME MY GUITAR HIS EYES LOOKED DARK AND MEAN

HE GOT STRAIGHT UP AND OUT THE DOOR HE WENT

FROM THE WAY HE WAS DRESSED YOU WOULDN'T

THINK HE HAD A SCENT

HIS HAIR WAS LONG AND STRINGY HIS BACK WAS LIGHTLY BENT

ALL ALONE WALKED UP THE ROAD I NEVER SEE HIM AGAIN

WHO WAS THAT OLD MAN I ASK, NO SEEM TO KNOW

JUST WHAT I WAS TALKING ABOUT AS HE EYED ME

HEAD TO TOE

NOBODY HERE BUT US YOUNG MAN SAID A GUY

IN THE SECOND ROW

THEY SEEMED TO THINK I'D LOST MY MIND

IN THEIR FACES IT DID SHOW

MUCH TIME I SPENT THINKING BOUT THAT OLD MAN I'D SEEN

THE SOUND OF THAT OLD GUITAR IN MY MIND AND HOW

THAT IT DID RING

NEXT NIGHT A MAN SAID THAT LOOKS LIKE GRANPA'S

OLD GUITAR IT SEEMS

WITH THOUGHTFUL WORDS HE DESCRIBED THE OLD MAN

THAT HAD PLAYED FOR ME

HIS WORDS DESCRIBED THE OLD MAN JUST PERFECTLY

HE SURE PLAYED THAT GUITAR FOR ME

THAT OLD MAN ONLY I HAD SEEN

TWO FINGERS

  D   G   D
ONLY TWO FINGERS LEFT STANDING IN THE BOTTLE

                                        D7
IT'S EARLY AND I DON'T THINK IT WILL LAST

                G   D
WHEN YOU LEFT I TOOK A SIP OF LIQUID COURAGE

                A   D
HERE I SIT THINKING OF THE PAST

D   G
OH YOU NEVER KNEW HOW MUCH YOU HAD ME
D
SPELL BOUND

                                                    D7
YOU NEVER KNEW MY STRENGTH WAS IN YOUR HAND

            G   D
OH YOU NEVER KNEW MY LIFE WAS BUILT AROUND YOU

                A   D
HERE I SIT THE BOTTLES' GOT YOUR MAN

YOU ARE OUT THERE THERE'S A PARTY EVERY WEEKEND

THE STORY'S COME TO ME MAN TO MAN

THEY SAY YOU'RE GOING TO THE PLACES THAT WE'VE BEEN

I'M TRYING TO FORGET YOU IF I CAN

OH YOU NEVER KNEW HOW MUCH YOU HAD ME SPELL BOUND

YOU NEVER KNEW MY STRENGTH WAS IN YOUR HAND
YOU NEVER KNEW MY LIFE WAS BUILT AROUND YOU
HERE I SIT THE BOTTLES' GOT YOUR MAN

DON'T LIVE YOUR LIFE WITH THE BRAKES ON

A-E-E-A- A-D-E-A
DON'T LIVE YOUR LIFE WITH THE BREAKERS ON
GET OUT THERE AND MOVE AROUND MY FRIEND
DO SOME THINGS YOU WANT TO DO
YOU'LL NEVER COME DOWN THIS ROAD AGAIN
NEVER SAY NEVER
IT WILL COME BACK AND HAUNT YOU AND THEN
YOU'VE LIVED YOUR LIFE WITH THE BREAKERS ON
AND MISSED OUT ON THINGS THAT COULD HAVE BEEN
H
LATER COULD BE BAD
IF YOU REALLY HAVE THE URGE TO GO
THE PENDULUM IN YOUR HEAD IS SWINGING
BACK AND FORTH FROM YES TO NO
GRAB HOLD OF THAT DREAM AND HANG ON
RIDE IT TO THE END
DON'T LIVE YOUR LIFE WITH THE BREAKS ON
YOU'LL NEVER COME BACK DOWN THIS ROAD AGAIN
HOLDING BACK IS EASY
THAT'S A WASTE OF COURAGE MY FRIEND
A LONG LIFE SEEMS SHORT
IF YOU HAVE ENJOYED WHERE YOU'VE BEEN
A SHORT LIFE IS LONG
IF YOU SIT BACK AND WATCH IT SLIP BY
DON'T LIVE YOUR LIFE WITH THE BREAKERS ON

YOU'LL NEVER MAKE THE GRADE IF YOU DON'T TRY
DON'T LIFE YOUR LIFE WITH THE BREAKERS ON
GET OUT THERE AND MOVE AROUND MY FRIEND
DO SOME THINGS YOU WANT TO
YOU'LL NEVER COME BACK THIS ROAD AGAIN
NEVER SAY NEVER IT WILL COME BACK AND HAUNT
YOU AND THEN
YOU'LL HAVE LIVED YOUR LIFE WITH THE BREAKERS ON
AND MISSED THINGS THAT SHOULD HAVE BEEN
DON'T LIVE YOUR LIFE WITH THE BREAKERS ON
YOU'LL NEVER COME BACK THIS WAY AGAIN

DON'T WALK ALONE

C
I WALK IN THE RAIN
I WALK IN THE SUNSHINE
D
WALK IN THE MEADOW
A
AND THE SAND DOWN BY THE SEA
C
I WALK IN THE MOONLIGHT
UNDERNEATH THE STARLIGHT
YOU THINK I WALK ALONE
E
BUT SOMEONE WALKS WITH ME

A MAN CAN WALK ALONE
AND LEAVE TWO SETS OF FOOT PRINTS
I SAW THAT IN A PICTURE
MANY YEARS AGO

IF YOU BELIEVE THAT
YOU'LL HAVE SOMEONE TO LEAN ON
OVER THE HILLS AND VALLEYS
OF LIFES LONESOME ROAD

CH

SEE THE NONBELIEVER
THEY DON'T UNDERSTAND THAT

AND STRUGGLE WITH JUST HOW THAT COULD BE

IF THEY OPEN UP THEIR HEART
AND READ FROM THE GOOD BOOK
THEY COULD ALSO MEET
THE MAN WHO WALKS WITH ME

GIRL WITH GOLD IN HER HAIR

D

I WAS WALKING ONE NIGHT IN THE CITY   **DGDA**
SHE WAS WORKING THERE
SHE WAS A MAID IN A BAR ROOM   **DGDAD**
GOLD GLITTER IN HER HAIR

UNHAPPY IT WAS APPARENT   **DGDA**
A TEAR SPARKLED IN HER EYE
COME HOME WITH ME I WILL TAKE YOU   **DGDAD**
WHERE NO ONE WILL MAKE YOU CRY

I'LL TAKE YOU TO MY HOME NOW GAGD
YES I WILL MARRY YOU THERE

THERE'LL BE NO TEARS IN YOUR EYE DEAR   **GDAD**
NO GOLD GLITTER IN YOUR HAIR

SHE SAID MISTER YOUR PICTURE IS PRETTY   **DADDAD**
BUT YOU DO NOT UNDERSTAND
I DO NOT WANT TO MARRY GDDAD
BUT FOR TONIGHT YOU CAN BE MY MAN

NOW MAMA HAD TOLD ME ABOUT IT   **DADDAD**
THIS PLACE I FOUND DOWN HERE
SAID SON DON'T LET IT CONSUME YOU   **GDDAD**
THE WILD WEMAN THE WHISKEY THE BEER

AFTER A NEAL AT NIGHTS BIG TABLE
I WENT BACK WHERE I CAME
I LEFT THERE WHILE I WAS ABLE

SPARED MY FRIENDS AND FAMILY MUCH SHAME

I CAN'T HELP BUT THINK TODAY NOW   **GDGDGDAD**
IF I WERE TO GO BACK THERE
WOULD SHE REMEMBER ME LIKE I DO HER
THAT GIRL WITH GOLD IN HER HAIR

GUNS GUITARS AND GIRLS

```
D                   A              D
LET'S TALK ABOUT GUNS GUITARS AND GIRLS
             A              D
TALK ABOUT GUNS GUITARS AND GIRLS
G                        D
GUNS ARE MADE FOR SHOOTING COWBOYS ROOTIN
TOOTIN
E                        A
GUITARS DRIVE THE MUSIC WORLD
            D     A     D
THEN YOU GOT GIRLS GIRLS GIRLS

D
SOME GUNS ARE MADE FOR KILLING
A
COMPETITION WITH BIG BILLING
D                                     G
PRETTY ONES WITH HANDLES MADE OF PEARLS
            D     A     D
THEN YOU GOT GIRLS GIRLS GIRLS
```

GUITARS THE BASE FOR COUNTRY MUSIC
ALL THE STARS HAVE HAD TO USE IT
MADE FOR FOLKS LIKE CHET DOC AND MERYL
THEN YOU GOT GIRLS GIRLS GIRLS
TALKING ABOUT GUNS GUITARS AND GIRLS
TALKING ABOUT GUNS GUITARS AND GIRLS

GUNS ARE MADE FOR SHOOTING COWBOYS ROOTIN TOOTIN

GUITARS ARE MADE TO DRIVE THE MUSIC WORLD

TALKING ABUT GUNS GUITARS AND GIRLS

TALKING ABOUT GUNS GUITARS AND GIRLS

GIRLS WITH WARM AND FUZZY FEELING

THEY WILL SET YOUR HEART A REELING

FAME AND FORTUNE IS REAL BIG IN THEIR WORLD

WE'VE TALKED ABOUT GUNS GUITARS AND GIRLS

PRETTY EYES AND ALL THOSE GIRLS

WE'VE TALKED ABOUT GIRLS GIRLS GIRLS

WE'VE TALKED ABOUT GUNS GUITARS AND GIRLS

GUNS GUITARS AND GIRLS

GUNS GUITARS AND GIRLS

GUNS ARE MADE FOR SHOOTING COWBOYS ROOTIN TOOTIN

GUITARS DRIVE THE MUSIC WORLD

THEN YOU GOT GIRLS GIRLS GIRLS

JUST AN OLD GUITAR

D
HERE I SIT IN THE CORNER
BEEN REPLACED BYY SOMETHING NEW
A
MY OLD SOUND NOT GOOD ENOUGH
    G   **D**
TO DO WHAT THEY MUST DO

D
NOT MANY YEARS AGO
NEARLY ANYTHING WOULD DO
A
JUST A SIMPLE CHORD
      G   **D**
OR A PRETTY RUN OR TWO

D
IN HISTORY ROY AND DALE WOULD SING THEIR COWBOY SONGS
A   **G**   **D**
JUST AS GENE AUTRY WOULD AS HE RODE ALONG

D
JIMMY ROGERS AND TEX RITTER KEPT IT SIMPLE AS COULD BE
A   **G**
BUT NOW I'M IN THE CORNER NOT QUITE GOOD

```
                D
ENOUGH YOU SEE
D
EDDIE ARNOLD AND HANK WILLIAMS SANG A
DIFFERENT KIND OF SONG
A                                    G
BUT LISTEN IN THE BACKGROUND MY MUSIC COMES
    D
IN STRONG
D
EVERY THING IS CHANGING NO MATTER WHERE YOU ARE
A                            G
I CAN SURE ATEST TO THAT AND I'M JUST AN OLD GUITAR
```

I MET AN OLD COW-HAND

A   D
WHILE TRAVELING OUT IN TEXAS I MET AN OLD COW-HAND
  A
HE TALKED ABOUT THE OPEN RANGE AND THE LIFE
 E
HE LED
  A   D
WAS YOU LONELY AS A DROVER AND THIS IS WHAT HE SAID
 A   E
IT'S HARD FOR ME TO TALK ABOUT AS HE SLOWLY
   A
BOWED HIS HEAD
A
THE YEARS HAVE GONE THE TIME HAS PASSED
 E
WHEN YOUNG I DID IT ALL
HOW WAS I TO KNOW THE DAY WOULD COME
   A
WHEN I'D TAKE THAT GREAT FALL
      D
NOW IT'S ONLY MEMORIES BUT NO LIFE WAS GOOD
A   E A
LONELY NEVER TALKED ABOUT OR EVEN UNDERSTOOD

D
THAT QUARTER HORSE WAS MY BEST FRIEND
    A
WHILE RIDING FENCE BY DAY
THE DOGGIES KEPT ME COMPANY AFTER HERDING
     E
UP THE STRAYS
A
GUITAR AND SONG AT CAMPFIRE TIME
    D
AS WE FINISHED UP THE DAY
  A
IF I COULD JUST TURN BACK THE TIME
    G   **A**
ON THE OPEN RANGE I'D STAY

YOU LEFT YOUR RING ON MY TABLE LAST NIGHT

A   **D**
I LEFT OUR HOUSE LATE YESTERDAY
A   **C**
LOOKED ALL AROUND NO REASON TO STAY
A   **D**
ALL ALONE IN THE DARKNESS WITH REALITY STING
       A   **E**
AS I PASSED BY THE TABLE MY EYES FELL ON THE
A
RING
A   **D**
THE RING YOU LEFT WAS MORE THAN I COULD BARE
         A   **E**
I COULD ONLY REMEMBER YOU AS YOU LEFT IT THERE
         A   **D**
YOUR LONG SLENDER FINGERS LILLY WHITE HAND
       A   **E**
THE SAME HANDS ON WHICH I PLACED YOUR WEDDING
A
BAND

       D   **A**
CH== YOU LEFT THAT RING ON MY TABLE LAST NIGHT
                   E
I'M HOPING YOU'LL RETURN AND MAKE IT ALL RIGHT

```
D                         A
YOU LEFT THE RING ON MY TABLE LAST NIGHT
                        E         A
I'LL ONLY BE HAPPY WHEN THE RING IS OUT OF SIGHT
A                   D
I KICKED AT THE TABLE AND PULLED AT MY HAIR
  A                       E
I TOOK ONE LOOK BACK SAW THE RING WAS STILL THERE
        A                 D
WENT OUT INTO THE DARKNESS AND IN MY DESPAIR
            A                   E
I THOUGHT BACK TO THE TABLE I KNEW THE RING WAS
A
STILL THERE

CH==

D                   A
I KNEW IT WON'T LEAVE A MARK ON YOUR HAND
                                E
CAUSE WE'RE NOT TALKING ABOUT YOUR WEDDING BAND
        A         D
THAT OLD OAK TABLE FOR EVER MAY STAND
          A               E       A
YOUR JACK AND COKE DRINK LEFT A RING LIKE A BAND
          A                   D       A
YOUR JACK AND COKE DRINK LEFT A RING LIKE A BAND
```

JUST RETURNED FROM A BATTLE

```
A                     D
HE SAT ON A STOOL WITH A CUP IN HIS HAND
        A                     E
AS HE STRADLED THE STOOL LIKE A SADDLE
   A                   D
THE COFFEE WAS BLACK AND STRONG LIKE THE MAN
         A      E        A
AS HE JUST RETURNED FROM A BATTLE

A                     D
SUNSET WAS NEAR AS HE GLANCED THROUGH THE DOOR
                              E
ARE THEY COMING TO TAKE ME DOWN
     A                   D
HIS MIND WANDERED BACK TO EARLIER THAT MORN
           A       E         A
AND THE COWBOYS HE LEFT ON THE GROUND

A                       D
SHE WAS THE REASON HE'D DONE SUCH AN ACT
         A              E
HER BEAUTY STRONG ON HIS MIND
A                    D
ONLY A FOOL WOULD HAVE DONE SUCH A THING
A            E
NOW THE END JUST A MATTER OF TIME
```

```
A                       D
THE DOOR SWUNG OPEN THE GUNFIRE WAS LOUD
A                       E
LIKE LIGHTNING HE SPUN ON A DIME
A                D
NOT FAST ENOUGH FOR THREE AS THEY FIRED
A      E      A
SOON IT WAS OVER THIS TIME

A                    D
HE SAT ON A STOOL WITH A DRINK IN HIS HAND
A                          E
AS HE STRADLED THE STOOL LIKE A SADDLE
A                    D
THE COFFEE WAS BLACK AND STRONG LIKE THE MAN
A        E         A
HE HAD JUST RETURNED FROM A BATTLE

NOW HE HAD FOUGHT HIS LAST BATTLE
```

IF YOU KNOW JACK

A
A LITTLE PLACE IN TENNESSEE
WHERE MOST FIND SERENITY
YOU'LL WANT TO COME BACK
    D
IF YOU KNOW JACK
    A
IF YOU KNOW JACK
    A
IF YOU KNOW JACK

YOU'LL WANT TO COME BACK
TWISTED TOP ON A PAPER SACK
SMELL THAT MASH YOU'RE ON THE RIGHT TRACK
    D
IF YOU KNOW JACK
    A
IF YOU KNOW JACK

CORN MASH BREWING YOU CAN SEE
AROMA FLOWING THROUGH THE TREES
YOU CAN TELL FOR SURE YOU'RE ON THE RIGHT TRACK
    D
IF YOU KNOW JACK
    A
IF YOU KNOW JACK

A
STANDING THERE DRESSED IN BLACK
TWISTED TOP ON A PAPER SACK
YOU KNOW ALL ABOUT THAT
      D
IF YOU KNOW JACK
      A
IF YOU KNOW JACK

IF YOU KNOW JACK
YOU'LL WANT TO COME BACK
TWISTED TOP ON A PAPER SACK
SMELL THAT MASH YOU'RE ON THE RIGHT TRACK
AND IF YOU DON'T WANT TO COME BACK
THEN YOU DON'T KNOW JACK

AND IF YOU DON'T WANT TO COME BACK
THEN YOU DON'T KNOW JACK

OLD WESTERN COWBOY

C-F-C-F-C-F-C-Am-C-G7-C

C   **F**   **C**
I'M JUST AN OLD WESTERN COWBOY
F   **C**
NOT MUCH MORE I CAN SAY
F   **C**   **Am**
I'M JUST AN OLD WESTERN COWBOY
C   **G7**   **C**
PUNCHING CATTLE ALL DAY

THEY ALL TOLD ME NOT TO DO IT
AT FOURTEEN I WENT ASTRAY
I KNIFED AN OLD DRUNKEN COWBOY
SO NOW OUT ON THE RANGE I MUST STAY

CAUSE I'M JUST AN OLD WESTERN COWBOY
NOT MUCH MORE I CAN SAY
I'M JUST AN OLD WESTERN COWBOY
PUNCHING CATTLE ALL DAY

C-F-C-F-C-F-C-Am-C-G7-C

OUT IN THE BADLANDS OF OLD MEXICO
THEY WILL CATCH ME SOME DAY
AND THAT'S WHERE I WILL BE BURIED
UNDER BOULDERS WEATHERED AND GRAY

I'M JUST AN OLD WESTERN COWBOY
NOT MUCH MORE I CAN SAY

I'M JUST AN OLD WESTERN COWBOY
PUNCHING CATTLE ALL DAY

SUNSHINE

> D   G   D

I'VE GOT SUNSHINE IN MY LIFE TODAY

CAUSE THE STORM CLOUDS

      E   A

HAVE UP AND PASSED AWAY

D

FAITH HOPE AND CHARITY

G   D

MAKES ME FEEL THIS WAY

        A   D

I GOT SUNSHINE IN MY LIFE TODAY

G

I FEEL LIKE TRAVELING DOWN THAT ROAD

     D

IN A CARE-FREE SORT OF WAY

 G

I DON'T CARE WHERE I'M GOING

A

DON'T KNOW HOW LONG I'LL STAY

 D

I SEE THAT SUN A-SHINING

  G   D

I SAY COME WHAT MAY

       A   D

I GOT SUNSHINE IN MY LIFE TODAY

I SEE NO NEED TO WORRY
AND FIGHT THAT UNDUE STRAIN
JUST NEED TO BE CAUTIOUS
NOT TO BE LED ASTRAY
FAITH IN THE LORD ABOVE
HOPE MY LUCK WILL STAND
WHEN YOU TALK ABOUT CHARITY
WE'LL LOOK TO OUR FELLOW MAN

I GOT SUNSHINE IN MY LIFE TODAY
CAUSE THOSE STORM CLOUDS HAVE UP
AND PASSED AWAY
FAITH HOPE AND CHARITY MAKES ME FEEL THIS WAY
I GOT SUNSHINE IN MY HEART TODAY

HONEY YOU CAN BEAT THAT

D

DOWN BY THE OLD FISHING HOLE BENDING POLE   **D**
                                        G
GRABBED A-HOLD IT WAS A BIG OLD CAT   **D-G**
HONEY YOU CAN BEAT THAT YAH YAH   **G-D**
HONEY YOU CAN BEAT THAT   **A-D**

D

BLUE JEANS COWBOY HAT

GUITAR STRAPPED ACROSS YOUR BACK
                             G
HONEY YOU CAN BEAT THAT

A   **D**
YAH YAH YAH HONEY YOU CAN BEAT THAT

CH==

D

UP ON THE MOUNTAIN THAT BEAUTIFULL SNOW

LONG SKIS AND CLIMBING POLE
                           G
HONEY YOU CAN BEAT THAT

D

HONEY YOU CAN BEAT THAT

D

YOU'RE SO HOT YOU CAN MELT THAT SNOW

SITTING ON READY AND RARING TO GO

          G
HONEY YOU CAN BEAT THAT

A   **D**

YAH YAH YAH YOU BEAT THAT

CH==

DOWN BY THE BEACH AND ALL THAT SAND

COLD BEER IN MY RIGHT HAND

HONEY YOU CAN BEAT THAT

HONEY YOU CAN BEAT THAT

STANDING THERE IN THAT TWO-PIECE SUIT

THE BOYS ALL THINK YOU'RE SO CUTE

HONEY YOU BEAT THAT

YAH YAH YAH HONEY YOU BEAT THAT

CH==

SITTING IN THE MEADOWS IN THE MORNING DEW

LOOKED IN MY EYES AND SAID I LOVE YOU

HONEY YOU CAN'T BEAT THAT

HONEY YOU CAN'T BEAT THAT

THOSE THREE WORDS COMING FROM YOU

BEATS ALL THE OTHER STUFF YOU CAN DO

HONEY YOU CAN'T BEAT THAT

NO NO NO YOU CAN'T BEAT THAT

SITTING IN THE MEADOW LOOKED IN MY EYES

SAID I LOVE YOU

HONEY YOU CAN'T BEAT THAT

NO NO NO CAN'T BEAT THAT

ROUTE 55 BLUES

G
GOING DOWN ROUTE 55
        C
THROUGH TENNESSEE AND SAKES ALIVE
      D
SEEN A BIG OLD SIGN JUST UP AHEAD
                      G
SOUR MASH WHISKEY IS WHAT IT SAID

G
TURNED IN THE PARKING LOT AND I COULD TELL
        C
WE WERE AT THE RIGHT PLACE BY THE ODOR I SMELLED
     D
SOUR MASH CLOSE FOR SURE SO WE WENT IN FOR
            G
OUR GRAND TOUR

G
WITH A TEAR IN OUR EYES AND SINUS CLEANED OUT
    C
THE TOUR GUIDE LEFT US WITH ONE BIG LAUGH
D
SO WE PRESSED ON TO THE LITTLE OLD TOWN
                         G
WHOSE NAME IS KNOWN THE WORLD AROUND
LYNCHBURG JUST ACROSS THE CREEK

AT THE FOOT OF THE HILL TOWERING SO STEEP
TAVERN IT'S CALLED YOU MIGHT KNOW WHY
THERE WAS A TAVERN UP THERE IN YEARS GONE BY

UP THROUGH THE ALLEY BEHIND THE BANK
THERE'S THE SIGHT OF A SKULL THAT WILL MAKE YOU THINK
A SHOP THERE RUN BY A LONG HAIRED DUDE
HE'S FROM GEORGIA BUT HE WON'T BE RUDE

OUT TO THE SQUARE ANOTHER IT IS
WHERE THE COURT HOUSE SAT FOR A HUNDRED YEARS
AND YOU CAN BUY MOST ANYTHING HERE
ANTIQUES GIFTS AND JACK DANIEL BEER

THE BBQ SMELL FROM THE CAFE CABOOSE
WHERE THE FINEST OF PORK IS WAITING FOR YOU
MUSIC IS PLAYED JUST INSIDE
BLUEGRASS AND COUNTRY IS PLAYED WITH PRIDE
BACK ON THE ROAD TO SOME BIGGER TOWN
BIGGER AND LOUDER MAY BE FOUND
BUT I BET YOU AIN'T SEEN NOTHING LIKE THIS

IT'S LYNCHBURG TENNESSEE AND LAID BACK BLISS

I-PHONE BLUES

 A   **E**   **E**   **G**
I GOT THE I-PHONE BLUES I GOT THE I-PHONE BLUES
D
PEOPLE SITTING ROUND WITH THEIR HEAD IN THEIR

APPS
A
FACEBOOK TWITTER AND GOOGLE MAPS
THEY GOT THE I-PHONE BLUES
A
EYES ON THE ROAD HANDS ON THE WHEEL
NOT ANY MORE AND IT'S A GREAT BIG DEAL
                  D
IT'S CALLED THE I-PHONE BLUES
A   **E**   **A**
THE I-PHONE BLUES I-PHONE BLUES
A
SITTING ROUND THE TABLE AND THE KIDS ALL TEXT
MAKES THE OLD FOLKS A NERVOUS WRECK
                D
THEY GOT THE I-PHONE BLUES

CH== A

WE DON'T KNOW WHAT'S NEXT IN STORE
BUT WE CAN'T STAND A WHOLE LOT MORE
            D
WE'LL HAVE THE I-PHONE BLUES

          A
WE'LL HAVE THE I-PHONE BLUES
      A
I-PHONE BLUES
A
HARD TO GET A GOOD NIGHTS SLEEP
WAKE EVERY TIME IT BEEPS
            D
YOU GET THE I-PHONE BLUES
         A   **E**   **A**
THE I-PHONE BLUES I-PHONE BLUES
A
SOMETIMES THE THING DON'T RING
JUST MAKES A FUNNY LITTLE PING
            D
YOU GET THE I-PHONE BLUES
            A
YOU GET THE I-PHONE BLUES
E   **A**
I-PHONE BLUES

ALL THAT STUFF YOU PUT ON THE WEB
MIGHT BE SAD WHEN IT COMES TO A HEAD
YOU'LL HAVE THE I-PHONE BLUES
YOU'LL HAVE THE I-PHONE BLUES
I-PHONE BLUES
ALL CONSUMED IN THE I-PHONE MOOD
JUSTIFYING A THING CALLED RUDE

IT'S THE I-PHONE BLUES
IT'S THE I--PHONE BLUES
I-PHONE BLUES

STANDING IN LINE FOR DAYS ON END
JUST TO GET A PIECE OF THE LATEST TREND
MUST BE THE I-PHONE BLUES
I-PHONE BLUES   I-PHONE BLUES

LEGEND OF A LITTLE MAN

D   A
THERE'S A LEGEND OF A LITTLE MAN
                                   D
MADE AN IMPRESSION THROUGH THE LAND
                               A
MADE A LITTLE WHISKEY WITH THE WATER
                            D
FROM THE CAVE WITH HIS OWN HAND

D   A
THERE'S A LITTLE TOWN CALLED LYNCHBURG
                            D
NESTLED IN THE TENNESSEE HILLS
            A
IN METRO MOORE COUNTY
                        D
AND HIS SPIRITSS ARE STILL HERE

        G   D
AS YOU NEAR IT EARLY IN THE MORNING
      E   A
THERE'S NO MISTAKING YOU ARE THERE
   D   A
THE AROMA CORN MASH BREWING
                    D
AS IS FILLS THE COUNTRY AIR

```
D                              A
IF YOU ARE TRAVELING YOU MUST GO THERE
                  D
AND YOU'LL FIND IT AS I SAID
                                    A
IT'S A LITTLE LAID BACK AND THEY ARE WHITTLING
                       D
OVER ON THE COURT HOUSE SQUARE

D      G              D
A LIFE-SIZE STATUE NEAR THE WATER
         E           A
AT THE CAVE IS WHERE IT STANDS
             D          A
PATIENTLY WAITING FOR THE PICTURE
                         D
YOU CAN TAKE WITH THE LITTLE MAN

D                          A
THERE'S A LEGEND ABOUT A LITTLE MAN
                               D
MADE AN IMPRESSION THROUGHOUT THE LAND
                      A
MADE A LITTLE WHISKEY WITH THE WATER
                   D
FROM THE CAVE WITH HIS OWN HAND

MADE A LITTLE WHISKEY WITH THE WATER
FROM THE CAVE IN JACK DANIEL LAND
```

WE WILL DANCE

```
A                             E
I SAW YOU STANDING THERE IN YOUR WHITE COTTON
GOWN
                                        A
YOUR HAIR ALL UP IN CURLERS WAS LIKE BEFORE
                        E
I SAW YOUR GLOWING SMILE AS I CAME THROUGH THE
DOOR
                                A
I KNEW SOON WE'D BE OUT ON THE TOWN

A         D            A
AND WE WILL DANCE AND WE WILL DANCE
         E          D
WE WILL DANCE WE WILL DANCE
         D                        A
WE WILL HOLD EACH OTHER CLOSE AS WE GLIDE
ACROSS THE FLOOR
           D                            A
WE WILL WATCH THE PEOPLE STARE AT THE SILVER
IN OUR HAIR
             D           A
BUT WE WILL DANCE WE WILL DANCE
A                        D
IT STARTED LONG AGO NEAR A LITTLE COUNTRY TOWN
```

        A
HER HAIR ALL UP IN CURLERS A WHITE COTTON GOWN

D   **A**
FARM FIELDS BY DAY HAPPY DREAMS AT NIGHT

    E   **A**
IN HER DREAMS SHE WOULD DANCE

A   **D**   **A**
SHE WOULD DANCE SHE WOULD DANCE

     E   **A**
SHE WOULD DANCE SHE WOULD DANCE

    D
THOUGH SHE WAS JUST A LITTLE GIRL

  A
HER MIND WAS IN A WHIRL

E   **A**
IN MIND SHE WOULD DANCE

A   **E**
FAR ACROSS THE LAND ON THE FARM HE WAS A MAN

          A
MUSIC ALL AROUND BUT NEVER DANCED

          E
ONE DAY HE MET THE GIRL WITH HER HAIR ALL UP IN CURLERS

    A
SHE LET HIM DANCE

A **D**   **A**
WE DID DANCE WE DID DANCE

```
E                              A
EVERYWHERE WE WENT WE WOULD DANCE
         D              A
TONIGHT OUT ON THE TOWN PEOPLE ALL AROUND
         E
WE WILL DANCE
         D                  A
TONIGHT OUT ON THE TOWN WITH PEOPLE ALL AROUND
         E           A
WE WILL DANCE WE WILL DANCE
```

COLORADO BLUE

A   D   A
I MET HER ON THE MOUNTAIN ONE BRISK OCTOBER DAY
HER LONG BLOND HAIR WAS WAVING AS THE COOL
              E
WIND CAME HER WAY
   A   D
WE NEVER SPOKE A WORK THOUGH WE HAD MUCH TO
A
SAY
                          E
OUR EYES MET NOW THAT FEELING I LONG FOR EVERY
A
DAY

     D
CH== THE EYES I REMEMBER WERE ONES THAT COULD
  A
BE TRUE
                      E   A
THE SAME AS THE SKY ABOVE, COLORADO BLUE
D
COLORADO BLUE
A
COLORADO BLUE
THE EYES I RECALL

```
E     A
COLORADO BLUE
A                                       E
I TURNED AND SHE WAS GONE THOUGH I WANTED HER
TO STAY
                                    A
I GOT HER NAME FROM A CALLING CARD A STRANGER
PASSED MY WAY
                                        D
THE WESTERN STATES WAS CALLING ME A YEARNING
TO BE FREE
A                                       E
THE LIFE OF WILD AND WOOLEY WEST MY FUTURE IT
         A
WOULD BE
A                                       E
RAMBLING FROM HERE TO THERE THE TIME WHERE DID
IT GO
                                    A
THIS LIFE I LEAD ALL ALONE MY AGE BEGAN TO SHOW
                                    D
RETURNING TO THE MOUNTAIN NOT KNOWING WHAT
I'D DO
       A                    E           A
MY LIFE ALWAYS HUNTED BY COLORADO BLUE
```

CH== THE EYES I REMEMBER ==

D
COLORADO BLUE
A
COLORADO BLUE
THE EYES I RECALL
      E   **A**
WERE COLORADO BLUE
A   **E**
KNOCKING ON THE DOOR LOOKING FOR A PLACE TO STAY
                              A
WHEN THE DOOR HAD OPENED I KNEW NOT WHAT TO SAY
                                 D
I'VE THOUGHT OF YOU FOR MANY YEARS HER EYES WERE FILLED WITH TEARS
      A   **E**
THOSE EYES WERE SURELY TRUE STILL COLORADO
A
BLUE

CH== THE EYES I REMEMBER ==
D
COLORADO BLUE
A
COLORADO BLUE
THOSE EYES THAT WERE SO TRUE
E   **A**
STILL COLORADO BLUE

SMELL OF WHISKEY

D G
I WOKE UP THIS MORNING
                                       D
WITH THE SMELL OF WHISKEY IN THE AIR
G
THOUGHT ABOUT THE OLD MAN
                            D
PLAYING CHECKERS ON THE SQUARE
G
TWENTY FOUR SEVEN
                  D
YOU CAN JOIN HIM THERE

BUT HE MOSTLY SITS THERE ALL ALONE
           A   **D**
WITH THE SMELL OF WHISKEY IN THE AIR
D   **G**   **D**
LYNCHBURG IN THE HILLS OF TENNESSEE
                                       A
THE PLACE WHERE FOLKS FROM ALL OVER LIKE TO BE
G   **D**
MOST FOLKS FIND PEACE AND QUIET THERE
                                  A
THIS LITTLE TOWN WITH THE SMELL OF WHISKEY IN
     D
THE AIR

```
D                    G
CHARCOAL VATS DRIPPING ON THE HILL

                                           A
FROM ALL OVER PEOPLE COME JUST TO SEE THE STILL
     G                                A
UP THERE SPECIAL FOLKS GET A CHANCE TO SHARE
G                                    A
BUT WE'RE ALL FREE TO SIT DOWN HERE AND SMELL
                        D
THE WHISKEY IN THE AIR
D                G                  D
ALL YEAR THE STEAM RISES THROUGH THE TREES
D                     A
THE AROMA FLOATING IN THE BREEZE
          G                              D
SOUR MASH IS BREWING WITH A SCENT THAT'S RARE
                                 A
MEANWHILE DOWN IN THE HOLLER THE SMELL OF
                   D
WHISKEY FILLS THE AIR
                      G          D
LIMESTONE WATER IS WHAT HAS TO BE
                                           A
STATUE OF OLD JACK STANDING THERE FOR ALL TO SEE
         G                         D
THE SPRING IS RUNNING FREELY OVER THERE
```

                A
ENJOY THE PRESENT VIEW AND SMELL THE WHISKEY
    D
IN THE AIR
D   **G**
I WOKE UP THIS MORNING WITH THE SMELL OF
          D
WHISKEY IN THE AIR
    G
HE'S STILL THERE THE OLD MAN PLAYING CHECKER
      D
ON THE SQUARE
G   **D**
GO BY AND SIT A SPELL THERE IS ANOTHER CHAIR
WHEN YOU LEAVE THIS TOWN YOU'LL REMEMBER
    A   **D**
THE LITTLE TOWN WITH WHISKEY IN THE AIR

www.ingramcontent.com/pod-product-compliance
Lightning Source LLC
LaVergne TN
LVHW041707060526
838201LV00043B/620